Nurse, Please!!
Fifty Incredible Years as a Rural Kansas Nurse

By Rose Holcomb, R.N.

Plevna Publishing, LLC
Kansas

Scripture quotations are from The Holy Bible, King James Version.

Copyright © 2002 by Rose Holcomb

Published by Plevna Publishing, LLC
8118 S. Avery Rd.
Plevna, KS 67568

Cover by Deanna Steiner
Photo credits: Rose Holcomb, photo archive: front and back covers; Olan Mills: back cover

Printing history:
1st printing: December 2002
2nd printing: February 2003

Printed in the United States of America

Publisher's Cataloging-in-Publication Data
Holcomb, Rose M. (Rose Mayree), 1927-
    Nurse, Please!! Fifty Incredible Years as a Rural Kansas Nurse / Rose M. Holcomb. – 1st ed.
    p. cm.
    ISBN 0-9724305-0-4

    1. Medicine - Biography   I. Title
    2. Nurses and Nursing
    3. Women - Biography
610.73 2002

My dream of becoming a registered nurse could never have been completed without help from the following people:

my parents, Leonard and Edith Bridgeman, for the financial help and encouragement to finish nurse's training;

my mother-in-law, Jessie, for caring for our four sons and supplying food while I worked as a nurse;

my sister, Charlyne, for buying a necessary watch with a second hand 55 years ago;

my husband and sons for living with a sleep starved wife and mom;

many, many nurse friends who helped make memories;

my son, Kyle, for assisting with the purchase and installation of computer, copier, and scanner for use in this project;

daughter-in-law Karla, for advice, encouragement, prodding, typing, and overseeing this undertaking;

Justin Geist, my friend, neighbor, computer whiz, and adopted grandson, for enlightening and educating me on computer technique and actually emailing the book and pictures to Karla in Chicago;

the doctors of Stafford Hospital that I worked with and learned from;

all Stafford Hospital employees who made working there so pleasant;

the hundreds of patients it has been my privilege and joy to care for;

and my nurse friends who helped me endure the difficult times and enjoy the good times.

TABLE OF CONTENTS

Book 1: Nurse's Training

Who Wants to be a Nurse?

Who would ever want to be a nurse? Why, why? Don't you know you have to work on weekends? Don't you know you might have to work holidays – even Christmas? Oh, you might have to deal with bloody messes and other gory nasty things. Are you sure you want to be a nurse? And the doctors – could you stand it if they yelled at you? Yes, I heard these things, but still decided to be a nurse. Why?

I feel God directed me into the field of nursing. In Proverbs 3:5,6, it says, "Trust in the Lord with all thine heart and lean not unto thine own understanding. In all thy ways acknowledge Him, and He shall direct they paths." Proverbs 16:9 reads, "A man's heart deviseth his way: but the Lord directeth his steps." Sometimes the direction of His leading is difficult to determine, with a very gentle nudge or a small light on an obscure path. Other times it is quite clear, like a door slamming, and another one swinging open. This one thing I am sure of --- God has led. Looking back over my life I can see how beautifully, wonderfully, lovingly God has led. I can see how different people have been used to make a difference in my life. Yes, God has led and I am grateful.

I would like to share a few of the many memorable experiences of the past 52 years of life as an R.N.

In the early 1930s I was living on the family farm in Reno County, Kansas with my parents and siblings. Life was simple. Our parents worked hard and we "kids" were

1

expected to help with chores. We raised cattle, hogs, sheep, turkeys, and chickens. All of these things were very important for our livelihood. One spring when I was a preschooler, our chickens were getting a good growth of feathers. One chicken got its wing caught in the woven wire fence. It was torn and bleeding when I found it. After freeing the poor injured chick, I was determined to restore it to health. We had some salve in a large, round, green tin which was supposed to cure every kind of injury because we rarely went to a doctor. I snuck it out to my first patient and smeared salve all over the chicken's wing. I was thrilled when the chick recovered, even though that wing drooped and the feathers didn't grow back properly. An idea and desire had been planted in my head and heart.

All through my school years, my goal and desire was to be a nurse. After preliminary schooling I headed for Wesley Hospital in Wichita. I was definitely a small town country girl, so with some apprehension, uneasiness, and excitement, I headed for the "big city". My parents took me to Hutchinson where I boarded a bus with the destination Wichita. Thus was the beginning of a career that has been interesting, exciting, happy, humorous, and sometimes sad. Nursing has seen many dramatic changes since that bus trip in 1947.

After getting off the bus in Wichita, I looked around, wondering where Wesley Hospital was and how to get there. While looking for a city bus stop, I noticed another young girl, carrying a suitcase and looking very uncomfortable in a pair of white, high-heeled shoes. We spoke to each other and realized we both wanted to get to Wesley, but neither of us knew how to get there. This Newton girl, another future nurse, and I found the proper bus that delivered us to the front of Burton Nurse's Home. I had found my new home, a friend and my roommate for the next three years. Upon arriving at Burton Home, we found that there were 50 eager, energetic, somewhat apprehensive young girls ready to enter the field of nursing. These gals were impatient to make an impact on the problems of the world. We were ready to heal the sick, eradicate disease, restore the injured, etc. We had no idea of the disappointments, setbacks, defeat, and death that lay ahead. Perhaps it was a good thing we were so optimistic, strong, and ready to do battle.

Our first five months of training were spent entirely in the classroom with a rather tough curriculum. We had to spend much time studying such subjects as chemistry, medical science, nutrition, anatomy and physiology, microbiology, pharmacology, and principles and practices of nursing. Now the last one mentioned was the one we were most eager for. You see, that was REAL nursing. After five months of intense studying, we would gradually get to begin caring for real patients. Those first five months it was surprising how quickly some of those so-called avid learners gave up and dropped out. Those of us who stayed the course not only became acquainted, but experienced a special bonding. Friendships grew and strengthened, with many lasting a lifetime. It seemed we were constantly drawn closer together with our testing, trials, tragedies, triumphs, and tears. Of course, we also had our fun times and would laugh uproariously at some of our foolish mistakes. Yes, we laughed together and cried together. It seemed each experience increased our bond of friendship. We discovered the rigors of nurse's training were more difficult than we expected.

Our first home was a very old, large, two-story frame house with a sprawling white porch and a large kitchen. It was truly a homey old place, though a probable fire hazard. Many a "probie" (apprentice nurse) experienced her first unforgettable days away from home behind the closed doors of this dear old house. Eight rooms had been added on to the house; these were much larger, brighter, and more pleasant. Everyone was hoping to be assigned to one of these much nicer rooms. The housemother greeted each arriving student with a smile, a kind word, and a very strict set of rules. She then gave us directions to our assigned rooms. When I told her my name, she informed me a room in the popular, coveted new addition had been reserved for me. WOW! Why? I found out that Mother Field and my Aunt Ruth were good friends. Without my knowledge, Aunt Ruth had thoughtfully helped make my first months away from home more pleasant.

Our classes were rather difficult, and our instructors insisted on formality. Of course, each class started with roll call, using only last names preceded by Miss. I still recall the order, because we heard it so often. Alley, Benjamin, Board, Bond, Brandt, Bridgeman, Carr, Carson, Engle, Feemster, Feldman, Garrett, Gibson, Graham, Holdeman, Holman, Kingsbury, etc. until Wight. Often, local physicians would assist with our education by hour-long lectures that were usually very worthwhile. Each time the doctor entered the classroom, all student nurses were to rise and "stand at attention". I think most of the doctors liked the respect this policy seemed to afford. One of our favorite doctors would wave his hand and tell us to sit down. He appeared embarrassed.

Many of the lessons and truths imparted by these wise instructors have made a lasting impression on me. Once, we were deep in the study of anatomy. We were impressed how tiny, minute, like cells would form tissues that in turn would unite and form organs. A group of organs would "cooperate" and become a system. All the systems of the body joined to form a human body. The deeper the study, the more staggering the concept. One of the student nurses asked the physician instructor how so many babies could be born so perfectly formed when it looked like so many things could go wrong in the formation process. His reply impressed me and remains in my thoughts. He said when you know the Creator and the wonderful perfect plan of creation, he marvels and is totally surprised when anything goes wrong. It reminds me of Psalm 139:14 which reads, "I will praise Thee; for I am fearfully and wonderfully made".

A big, very important moment came for all the gals who endured the grueling academic schedule and did not fail their finals. Each was issued a stiff blue uniform with board-like white collars and cuffs. Then, one of the most exciting and important events of our training occurred. In an impressive ceremony, with our families and friends in attendance, we received our caps. Each of us carried a lighted candle, and the director of the nursing school pinned our prized caps in place. How happy and proud we were. We often called it our "dignity". Now, at last, we were ready to start being a nurse, a real nurse. The time we spent on the "floor" was rather brief, however, because there were still so many classes and subjects to conquer.

I still remember many of my "firsts". The first patient I bathed was a man – we were all hoping for a female. A male also received my first enema. My first experience with catheterizing a patient – who would it be but an R.N.? Oooh! She knew so much and I was so inexperienced, but she knew it was my initiation. She was very sweet and actually talked me through it.

We began to value experience as a great teacher. We practiced and practiced so we could become nurses Wesley would be proud of. Wesley hospital was founded on Christian principles and in 1947 had very strict moral codes for the nursing school students. Dorm hours were difficult to abide by. Everyone was to be in by 10 o'clock and doors locked. One rule that was more easily broken was lights out by 11:00 p.m. Marriage was not allowed. I guess they thought divided attention was not conducive to the rigors of training necessary to produce the caliber of nurses they expected to graduate. Each day began at least by 6:00 a.m., with breakfast at 6:30. No one was allowed to skip this first meal of the day. Promptly, at 6:45 a.m., *every* student nurse was to be present in chapel for fifteen minutes set aside for a time of devotions to prepare our hearts for service to God and patients. There could be no better way to begin our busy days. Most of the time we gals were called on to lead chapel services each morning. We all enjoyed singing a hymn or two. One of the favorites was "Are Ye Able?" We often wondered if we were. Occasionally, because of days off or girls scheduled for the evening or night shift, we had problems finding a piano player. Phyllis Bond could play one song, "Wonderful Words of Life". It seems we sometimes sang that song often.

Shortly after beginning "floor" duty, we had a rude awakening. Nurses had to work weekends, Christmas, and all other holidays. We felt they picked on us and took advantage of our status as students. At least on Christmas and Easter we were served bacon for breakfast. We frequently found ourselves murmuring and complaining about the meals we were served.

We all tried to make Christmas a really special time even though most hearts were dreaming of home. Burton Home provided a huge tree and all available girls helped decorate it while Clarice Graham played carols on the piano. On Christmas morning we had orders to report to the floor at 5:30 a.m. in full uniform for caroling. We were aghast that they actually demanded us to rise at 5:00 a.m. to wake up sick people with our singing! We were each handed a lighted candle. The halls remained very dark. We slowly proceeded to walk all the halls of four floors singing all the familiar carols. The response from patients was tremendous. We immediately had a changed attitude. This tradition became the highlight of the year for us.

One incident concerning our Christmas tradition remains strong in my memory. After we had caroled down the halls with our candles and had our festive special breakfast, we began our morning assignment of patient care. I began bathing and caring for my first patient, an elderly, frail man who was quite ill. He immediately began to excitedly tell me of this wonderful experience he had had in the wee hours that morning. He reported about the most unusual, beautiful occurrence. You see, he heard the angels sing that morning. They sang, "Joy to the World". There was a candle that lit each angel's face with a white thing over their head. "I guess it was a halo." I didn't have the heart to tell him what he saw was only a bunch of nurses. He was overjoyed because he finally got to see some real angels and hear their beautiful singing! Imagine! None of us were very good singers, but it certainly made one person happy. The next morning when I reported for work, I was informed my frail, old patient had died, but I'm sure he died happy.

Classroom work continued to consume most of our time. We were not to spend more than eight hours a day nursing, including hours in class. Most of us were happy to be allowed to work on the floor. The most difficult times were when we reported to a floor at 8:00 a.m., were assigned to care for eight patients, then still had to report for class at 11:00 a.m. The instructors accepted NO excuse for being late to class. We rushed through baths at breakneck speed because we HAD to finish all baths and NOT be tardy to class in another building. During these times, we were frustrated, embarrassed, and rather sad about the quality of care given. Of course, this was not routine, but it did happen a little too often to please us.

Each time we were required to do a new procedure, an instructor or senior nurse would be at our side to supervise, offer moral support, or perhaps cause nervousness because of our inexperience.

As we began to have fewer hours with our heads and minds in search of medical wisdom, we were required to start rotations through all the special services. Thus we were supposed to be educated and knowledgeable in all aspects of nursing. With a name that began with B, I was usually one of the first to "break the ice". Some of these rotations lasted only a week or so, including the first, which was the diet kitchen. I thought this was a bore. The main thing we learned was the old (new to us), dumb waiter. This wonderful gadget brought prepared food from the main kitchen in the basement to all five floors. This was of special interest to poor, hungry student nurses, who knew the kitchen was securely locked after the evening meal was served. Our class had a wonderful variety of personalities, even some very brave, daring ones. They devised a system whereby a snack would be available after 10:00 p.m. On a floor with the least chance of detection, they would call the dumb waiter with the use of a button. One of the smaller, lighter gals crawled on the apparatus. Her cohort would close the door and send it to the basement where all the food was stored. Giving the nervy student time to obtain bread, cheese, fruit, or what was easily accessible, the accomplice would then bring the dumb waiter back to the floor. I enjoyed a cheese sandwich more than once before I found out how it became available. I would never have been brave enough to take the "ride" or push the buttons. I'm sure some promising, young, foolhardy nurses would have been expelled had they been discovered.

A big step in accepting responsibility was learning to pass out medications. Our instructors were eager to fill us with horrible, frightening stories of medication errors which ended in dire results. I often wondered if they were really true or just a method of making us especially careful.

To my knowledge, no one in our class made a grave mistake, but of course, we were an exceptional class. Ahem!

Surgery

The first major special service we encountered was surgery. Anticipation, excitement, hard work, being on call - we were eager and ready - we thought. Prior to an actual operation, there is much preparation. Our surgical instructor was a rather imposing figure. She was trim, pretty, neat, experienced and very professional. She taught us sterile technique like a drill sergeant in the army. Ten-minute hand scrubs with surgical soap and a brush had to be done properly under her close inspection. We practiced opening a surgical pack and donning a sterile gown and gloves without contamination over and over under her watchful eyes. My, but she could yell, scold, and reprimand. All she demanded was perfection. We learned if our sterile, gloved hands dropped below our waist, the sterile field was broken. We soon learned why this wonderful instructor was so demanding and tough. When we actually were scrubbed in to assist a surgeon and got yelled at, she was our advocate. She really stood up for "her girls". Each student nurse was to scrub for 25 minor and 30 major surgeries before moving on to the next area of service. It was at this time we became aware of the impatience and tempers of some physicians. Some surgeons simply did not like to continually have learning students on their team. Other M.D.s showed great patience and understanding. Oh, how we appreciated them.

One morning I was assigned to assist with a very delicate eye surgery. I was nervous upon seeing an eyeball removed from its normal resting place, but I was also quite fascinated and became absorbed in the proceedings. The doctor asked me for a special suture. The needle and suture were exceedingly tiny. In my haste to quickly please this doctor, the suture became frighteningly tangled. That doctor was so kind and patient. He said, "We aren't in a hurry, just take a deep breath, take your time, and work the tangle out." I did and the operation continued in an orderly fashion. Oh, how I loved that doctor.

There was a group of three surgeons who were all extremely difficult to please. No student nurse wanted to scrub for them, even though they were excellent surgeons. It had to happen; one morning the lot fell on me. In spite of a cranky doctor and my presence (what a combination), the operation was going very well, until ... suture time! I guess sutures were my downfall. Sutures were contained in sterile fluid within a glass tube about the size of a ballpoint pen. The glass was scored around the center to facilitate breaking it open. The scrub nurse, (me) was to take several four by fours (gauze), break the suture open, place it on the requested proper needle, and hand it to the doc. This awful day, when I broke the suture open, it left a jagged piece of glass which cut my hand. I was not aware of this at first, but the eagle-eyed doctor saw my glove fill up with very unsterile blood. He yelled; he screamed; he swore; he ranted and raved. He said I was not sterile and was contaminating the surgical field. He not only ordered me out of the room but didn't want me to ever return. And right then, I didn't want to ever enter any operating room again. I didn't know where to go to regain my composure. I ended up in the sterilization room because no one should be there. I sat down on a stool and shed copious amounts of tears. That was the first of many times I wondered why I

11

wanted to be a nurse. An older nurse who witnessed this episode knew where to find me. She came in to my sanctuary, put her arm around my shoulders, encouraged, and comforted me. I did not know who she was, but that act of kindness made a great impression on me and made a difference in my life. It was then I determined to give a word of encouragement and a friendly pat on the shoulder to a fellow human being who was hurting.

Actually, as I think back on my operating room experiences, it wasn't too bad. One of my classmates, Helen Carr, fainted during her first surgery assignment. It was this type of thing that caused several girls to decide nursing wasn't for them. But not Helen! No, she was determined to be a nurse. So back she went. About the time the scalpel separated the skin on the initial incision, Helen hit the floor. Some people suggested another profession. Not Helen; you see she knew she wanted to be a full-fledged nurse. Back she went. This time everyone was waiting for the inevitable to happen. It did. But Helen conquered and became a fine nurse. I might say she was not a surgical nurse, but practiced her profession many years, retiring in 1993. This world might be a better place if more people had the persistence and determination to attain their goals.

Two O.R. happenings remain in my memory. One was assisting with brain surgery, which was not nearly as common then as it is now. Although it didn't make me ill, I will admit it bothered me a bit to see farm-like instruments used to bore holes and saw through the skull to expose the brain. The other was an amputation.

One morning I was called on to help with an amputation. My job was to support the limb which was being removed. Every thing was fine and going well until I found myself holding a body part which was not connected to a living person. It became unbearably hot with my gown, cap, mask, and gloves on. I had a sick feeling envelope my entire body. I was determined I would not pass out. I was so relieved when the circulating nurse did her job and removed the limb to send it to the lab. Wow, I made it.

Several years later I assisted with the amputation of a toe. It was a rather simple operation performed quickly. Once again I was supporting the toes while the doctor did the amputation. Totally unexpectedly, I experienced the exact same feeling of my first amputation. And it was only a toe!

We were required to take our turn being on call for emergency surgery. We were expected to be available to report to surgery in three minutes. Sometimes, demands seemed unreasonable. Once again, we heard these stories of a life being saved because the surgery nurses got prepared for the emergency in such record time. Therefore, we had to remain very close to "home base".

After we had had some surgical experience, Bond and I (always the "B" girls) were scheduled to take call. Most of our call backs were for an appendectomy or to remove a foreign object from an infant's lung. One specialist hated popcorn and peanuts. Interesting things seem to happen on Saturday nights. Sure enough, about 9:00 p.m. one Saturday night, we got the call. It is strange how some things can remain in memory so vividly. I can close my eyes and still see this large man on a gurney covered with a white sheet which was becoming saturated with blood. This man had shot himself in the abdomen and was swearing loudly, because he wanted to die. He wanted us to leave him alone. His wife and children timidly and fearfully followed at a distance. We began surgery shortly after 9:00 to repair extensive damage. All his abdominal organs had been torn or lacerated by this shotgun blast. The liver was especially difficult to repair because of its rich blood supply that bleeds so easily. The stomach and spleen were easier to handle. Then there were the yards and yards of intestines with its fecal content spewed throughout the area. Chances of infection were almost certain, if he survived the surgery. We finally finished this lengthy procedure about 5:00 a.m. It was then we discovered that this man abused both his wife and his children. It seemed ironic. The patient wanted to die. The wife wanted him to die. The children wanted him to die. So the doctors and nurses stayed up all night working very hard so he would not die. He lived. Phyllis Bond and I were exhausted when we finally returned to the nurse's home. We didn't want to awaken our sleeping roommates at 5:15, so we went into the bathroom, sat on the hard cold floor, leaned against the wall, and wondered how we could report back to work in such a short time. We felt utterly drained. When the surgery director discovered that we had not been to bed, she excused us from duty the rest of the day. How thankful we were.

Each student nurse had her own special memories of her tour of duty in surgery. Some of these were shared and thoroughly enjoyed by all of us. Joan Whitaker had an experience which delighted the entire class. Joan was very intelligent, studious, shy, timid, and mild-mannered. She was just beginning her time in surgery, learning to be a scrub nurse. After a ten-minute scrub with brush and soap, carefully putting on sterile gown and gloves, the scrub nurse would prepare the instrument table. Next, she would help the surgeon into his gown, keeping everything sterile. Next came gloves for the surgeon. The nurse would open the sterile package of gloves, remove them and hold them for the doctor who could not touch the outer part of the glove. The nurse would pull the cuff wide apart and the doctor quickly thrust his hand into the powdered glove. Beautiful! Fun! There was one big, powerfully-built surgeon who resembled a wrestler. He delighted in seeing how much force and strength he could muster into that thrust into the glove. No hand was to go below the waist or the sterile field was broken. All students had been warned. We all learned how to spread the cuff apart and brace ourselves for that mighty thrust. So here was slightly built Joan assisting this "wrestler surgeon" in one of her first operations. She was determined to do a good job. She pulled the cuff wide apart and braced herself. This gruff, mean-tempered doctor, with a gleam in his eye, raised his arm and with all his strength, powered his hand into the waiting glove. Alas, Joan was ready but the poor glove couldn't take it. The glove parted company with the cuff. Joan had braced herself quite well, enabling her to release the greatest uppercut ever delivered in any operating room. The doctor was quiet, perhaps stunned. Joan was mortified. Everyone else loved it. Each time the incident was recalled it brought roars of laughter from her classmates.

Getting through surgical training was perhaps the biggest hurdle of all. It seemed to prepare us for much of what lay ahead.

Birth Rooms

With great anticipation, we approached our next special service, the birth rooms. Following a brief explanation of what our duties would be in actual deliveries, we were assured we would witness one delivery before we would assist the doctor with one. Ah, that sounded simple enough. But guess what? My first day, I had just entered the birth room suite when I was greeted with a few quick orders. There were two delivery rooms and three O.B. patients ready to deliver at the same time. The department head yelled at me to get into room one, scrub up and assist the doctor. WOW! This happened to be the kindest, most patient doctor on the staff. (I think.) Everything went beautifully. I had my first thrill of hearing a newborn's first cry. Many deliveries later I still experience a thrill, a sense of excitement, and a sense of satisfaction in witnessing this miracle of life.

Looking back on these mid-century years in our country, it becomes very evident how far our priorities and morals have declined. At that time, babies were allowed to remain in the womb and be born into a world ready to receive them. Working in O.B. was a happy, pleasant experience. Of course, there were sad moments, which usually occurred when babies did not survive. There were four maternity floors and the nurseries were almost always full with bawling but healthy infants. Now, unborn babies are disposed of to please a selfish society.

Many things that occurred during this time I don't feel free to write about. There were funny, embarrassing, hilarious, and disgusting events which happened. One time the O.B. doctor was intoxicated and acted in a very unprofessional and cruel manner. He lost the respect of many nurses that morning.

One regularly appearing O.B. patient came from a prominent Wichita family. About every year or two she would appear and deliver another baby girl. Her husband was determined to have a male heir. She was my patient when she gave birth to another sweet little girl. Her reaction and words surprised me. After hugging and loving her newborn female, she smiled and said, "Well, I'd better get home and go shopping for some new maternity clothes." What an attitude!

It was during this period of my training that I opened my big mouth and the wrong thing came out. (That frequently happened. Why couldn't I learn?) I was admitting a patient who was in labor. She was about my age (young at that time). An elderly, gray-haired man knocked on the door asking to see her. I turned to my patient and asked if it was okay for her father to come in. Rather sharply, she informed me that was her husband. Surely, I had learned a valuable lesson. Not so. Several years later, I again jumped to the wrong conclusion. I referred to the man accompanying a woman as her husband. This time it wasn't her husband but a very special friend. Her husband was elsewhere, probably with the kids at home.

Bill and Frances were a happily married couple who were quite devoted to each other. They were eagerly awaiting the birth of their first child. The due date was still two months off, when complications arose. Frances had toxemia and became eclamptic. Her blood pressure was fearfully high and she was very edematous over her entire

17

body. There was danger she might begin having seizures which would be fatal to both mother and baby. She was placed in the quietest room available and we kept it darkened. She was to have absolute quiet lest convulsions start. Frances was the only patient assigned to me. She, Bill and I had some wonderful, warm conversation as we spent several hours together. No other visitors were allowed. I had so much to learn about people. I was encouraged about her condition and thought we might win this battle. Then her sister appeared at the door, demanding to see Frances. I quietly explained that she had to be extremely quiet and could not receive visitors. I was totally unprepared for the small explosion that followed. I was informed that no blankity-blank student nurse would keep her from seeing her sister. The only way to stop her was with a football tackle, but I didn't think of that quickly enough. Very shortly thereafter, the supervisor successfully escorted her from the room. How thankful I was when no seizures occurred. Later that night, after I was off duty, her condition deteriorated. The doctor thought the only chance of saving the life of the mother was to do a C-section. Even that was unsuccessful. Frances and her baby died. I was glad I was not present when it happened because I had never been with anyone when death occurred. This one would have been especially difficult. Two days later when my shift ended, I entered the elevator to leave the birth room area. The only other person to get on the elevator was none other than Bill. He had returned to get his wife's watch that had been left in the room when she expired. Once again my inexperience was evident and rather glaring. He said he really had wanted to see me. He cried when he told me I was Frances' favorite nurse. I didn't know what to do or say. I cried, too, but wasn't really able to tell him she was my favorite patient. I couldn't talk so I just touched his hand. When the elevator reached the ground floor, we each stepped out and went our separate ways, never to meet again. A thought returned. Why did I decide I would be a nurse?

Most of the experiences in the O.B. area were happy and pleasant. It always seemed to be a busy, bustling place. What a joy to place a newborn into the arms of a proud and beaming mother. It was fun to hold very new babies, usually squalling and red, sometimes with rather pointed heads, for admiring friends and relatives to see through the nursery window. Watching their antics and expressions could be very entertaining and humorous.

Our time spent in the nursery was often quite tiring. There were almost always 20 or 25 babes occupying those little cribs. I cannot recall a time when there were 25 kids sleeping at one time, but often there were 25 loudly howling infants. We would start at one end changing diapers and proceed down the line. By the time we reached the other end the first one would be wet, messy, (I do mean MESSY), and crying.

Some people say all babies look alike, but not so! We would have pet names for each baby, according to the way they looked. I remember two especially well. One we called a truck driver, the other one a pugilist. The names usually foretold their occupation, in our imagination. It was entertaining and helped us tolerate the noise of hungry or uncomfortable babies.

We had much to learn about caring for tiny, newborn babies, some of which were terribly important for serious reasons, others of which were important for the comfort of the nurse. One rather nice policy of the O.B. department was to have a student nurse demonstrate proper care of an infant, including actually bathing one of the little ones. The mothers would gather in a special room near the nursery and sit directly in front of the nurse. I think each new mother wondered if the nurse would choose the absolutely cutest, most precious baby in the entire hospital for the bath demonstration. Each mother leaned forward eagerly to see if it might possibly be her little miracle of conception. We very quickly learned to always choose a babe of the female gender. You see, little boys invariably displayed their unique water works system, and sprayed the nurse, a mother, or himself. With gasps, giggles, and apologies, the show went on. One time and the lesson was learned! (Alas, God later entrusted me with four little boys requiring baths. I got good at ducking when necessary.)

Seeing and caring for seriously malformed infants was difficult and sad. I was not present at this delivery, but how well I remember our instructor telling all of us students that a baby had been born that night. It was dead, but she wanted all of us to go see the body because it was what she called a monstrosity (a severely malformed baby). Now we would be able to function properly and handle the situation if one was born on our shift. Maybe it helped, but I'm not sure. I could never really be prepared for the babies born with cleft palate, cleft lip, spina bifida, hydrocephalus, or microcephalus. I could later care for them with no problem, but that initial shock was always there. Once an infant was delivered and had only one-half a face. One side was perfectly formed with an eye, ear, half a nose and mouth. There was nothing on the other side, it was just flat. The doctor gasped and said, "Oh, No" when the baby began to breathe. Death came within the hour.

We should never underestimate the power and tremendous possibilities for achievement instilled within the human spirit. I was present at the birth of a little girl who was minus one hand and a portion of her arm. It appeared to be a real tragedy, but I have been privileged to get an occasional glimpse of her accomplishments. Her mother provided her with a very positive attitude. When the girl was quite young, she didn't seem to even know she was handicapped. She excelled in school, played the piano, was a cheerleader and a popular student. The classmates accepted her, hardly realizing she was minus a very important and useful body part. She is now a happy, successful mother and wife.

On another occasion, things did not have such a pleasant result. An infant afflicted with spina bifida was born to a young couple. After first gently preparing the mother about the birth defect of her baby, we carried the little one to her. It was wrapped in a blanket and face, hands, etc. appeared fine. But we had to uncover the baby to expose the back. This mother did not handle the situation well at all. She drew back, gasped, turned her head, and became ill. We removed the infant, wanting to give her time to adjust to the situation. We wanted her to learn to feed the baby, and begin to care for it. But each time the infant was taken to her, she exhibited the same reaction. The grandmother came in regularly every day and fed the baby. She was so tender and gave so much care and attention to the baby. She encouraged her daughter to no avail. The mother was dismissed from the hospital without ever touching her baby. The baby was later dismissed to the grandmother's care. We never heard the outcome of this case, but always hoped the mother would eventually care for her little one.

After spending many days in the birth rooms, nursery, and O.B. patient rooms, we had to put in one whole week working in the formula room. Mixing and sterilizing bottles of correctly prepared formula for 70 to 80 infants was the most uninteresting, boring place I worked. We all felt like the hospital was merely using us for free labor. Of course, all of that was soon obsolete, with companies coming out with pre-mixed formulas already bottled and sterile.

Emergency Room

Ah, yes, after gaining experience in giving medications, in surgery, in obstetrics, and nursery, it was thought that we were now ready for the excitement of emergency room trials. The E.R. supervisor was named Forgie, and she was the calmest, most unflappable person I have ever known. She spoke slowly, and could remain calm in the most tense situations. It was comforting to know we would learn under the watchful eye of this nurse. The interns enjoyed bossing the students and throwing their weight around. They certainly couldn't do it with Forgie.

Children were frequent E.R. visitors. We had to deal with dog bites (some of them gruesome), numerous lacerations, and ingestion of very strange things. Kids swallowed pins, safety pins, tacks, coins, ink, paint, mothballs, all sorts of cleaning supplies, and adult medications. It was at this time I first heard the little ditty sung by Jackie Wight. It went like this, "Ah ha, Santi-flush, cleans your teeth without a brush."

Gun shot wounds, stab wounds, and serious injuries from auto accidents were difficult for me. Could we ever be really prepared for what we might encounter? Occasionally, the injuries were such that we actually felt ill. Some of my classmates had to exit vomiting. I was fortunate to be able to remain in the room and try to assist in care. One of the worst for me was a man who was in a car wreck. He had severe head injuries, with much blood. When I realized the large pieces of tissue on the face and skull were really his brain, that about did me in.

Several things happened to people while they were doing immoral things. Necessity required a hospital visit to the emergency room. I still cannot bring myself to relate these things. Perhaps I am a prude, but it seems vulgar, filthy, and embarrassing to me, to consider writing of these things. Forgie, our E.R. supervisor, handled all these episodes in such a calm, cool manner. It seemed nothing ever shocked her. I tried to emulate her. Even if I was utterly aghast, I tried to hide it. We were taught not to judge people, but to treat all with compassion.

During my E.R. stint I was confronted with my first real test of holding in confidence all personal matters committed to my keeping. This was one thing that was constantly hammered into our minds. One of my classmates, who was on duty in surgery, was brought into the emergency room. She was definitely not functioning properly. The pupils in her eyes were pinpoint. Her speech was slurred. The attending physician was searching for the problem and became suspicious. Sure enough, the anterior aspects of both thighs showed needle marks. In surgery, the drugs were not checked as religiously as elsewhere because they were rarely used. This foolish, curious girl had tried morphine sulfate with drastic results. The director of the nursing school was called in for consultation. I can still see the piercing, steady gaze of the doctor into my eyes as he said, "You will tell NO ONE about this." I didn't until right now, and even now I will not write her name. My classmate very quietly and abruptly left nurse's training the next day. All the other girls in our class were completely surprised at the sudden departure of a promising nurse. Many questions were raised; no answers ever found. It has now been 45 years. I wonder what ever happened to this former classmate.

Pediatrics

Ah, at last, we were to begin a field of nursing I knew I would enjoy! Once again, ignorance is bliss. We had no idea what lay ahead. Since I loved kids and babies, I supposed I would find pediatrics the most enjoyable phase of nurse's training. Not so! Little did we realize that Wesley hospital would be the center for so many critically ill, malformed, severely injured children. I was not prepared to see and care for so many terminally ill kids.

One of the top five plastic surgeons in the U.S. worked at Wesley. When he was a young boy, a horse kicked him in the face, and he suffered rather severe facial injuries. He felt disfigured, but was such a kind, loving man, that people hardly noticed the scars. He devoted his life to restoring faces, and making them more presentable. From all over the country, parents brought babies born with cleft palate and cleft lip to Wesley for this gentle man to work his "magic". He was very particular about the post-op care of his little patients. As each of us student nurses began our work in his unit, he instructed every one individually, and fully expected perfect results. If there was ever a surgeon we all tried especially hard to please, it was this man. He was so particular and cared for each baby with such love and tenderness. Full restoration usually required three separate operations. The hope and expectation of this doctor was that no one would be able to tell that this child had been born with such a serious deformity. This was one of the bright spots in the pediatric ward.

There was another surgeon who brought numerous youngsters to Wesley from all over the state of Kansas. This doctor was at the head of the Kansas Crippled Children League. This orthopedic surgeon reminded us of a big grizzly bear. He appeared gruff, rough, and actually looked more like a wrestler than a surgeon. Looks were deceiving because he was quite good at fixing up little kids' malformed legs and arms. He loved them and they eagerly returned that love. Many, many of these children had to return every summer for follow up surgery or new cast fittings. Many of these young ones came from poor homes where parents were not concerned with cleanliness. We soon learned the first thing to do upon the arrival of these kids in the summer was to treat them for head lice. This, too, proved to be one of the happier aspects of pediatrics. We could see the improvement in functions of these kids and we knew that with each trip to the hospital, life was a little better for them. Really, that's what nursing was all about.

Even though these two physicians provided a bright spot in the pediatric wards, there was an unexpected sad side to this area of nursing. The warning came on one of my first days in pediatrics. Approaching the desk one morning, we noted a young pediatrician sitting down with his head on the desk quietly weeping. We certainly were not used to anything like this. He was trying to prepare himself before informing parents that their daughter had an untreatable, cancerous tumor.

Numerous times we were instructed not to become emotionally involved with our patients. How could we care for little children without showing them love and becoming "emotionally involved"? Immediately, I broke this rule. A three-year-old girl was in the hospital suffering from a

Wilms' tumor. This is a malignant growth on the kidney which usually makes its appearance early in life. This child was precious and thrived on attention. She was very quiet throughout her suffering. Her entire body filled with fluid and she was very swollen. Although there were only tiny slits where her eyes were, she managed to continue to see. It was summer time and all the kids on which the orthopedic surgeon had operated were encouraged to play on outdoor playground equipment. I held my little patient near a window on fifth floor so she could see the action down below. She was so quiet, but seemed to love it. Because of all the excess fluid, she was very heavy and my arms became so tired, but I stayed there as long as I could. Selfishly, I was thankful I was not present when she died. When my classmate came back to the nurse's home and informed me our little patient was gone, we sat down and cried together. I admired the patient, loving mother and enjoyed visiting with her.

Several other youngsters left a mark on my heart. A ten-year-old twin boy developed a malignant brain tumor which claimed his life. A family outing on Memorial Day to a cemetery ended tragically when a huge tombstone tipped over on a young lad, causing a head injury which eventually ended in death. There were many with incurable diseases that resulted in long, lingering weeks of suffering before death occurred. This part of training was not the fun, happy place I had anticipated.

Child abuse and neglect were much less prevalent then than they are now. At least it was seldom publicized. My first experience with neglect took place while I was working in pediatrics. A policeman found a seven-year-old girl rummaging through a garbage bin behind a grocery store. She was chewing on some moldy bread. Her little body was extremely thin and emaciated. Her eyes were sunken into her face; her hair hadn't been washed, brushed, or combed for days or weeks. The condition of her skin showed the same neglect. She was very fearful of everyone when she was admitted into our unit by the police. I was assigned to her care and was so eager to show her the love she must have been missing. I was advised to move very slowly. We started with a nice warm bath which was apparently a new experience for her. My gentleness and soft words brought no verbal response, only fear in her eyes. The doctors felt she was nearly starved and wanted her to have food before any examination. We were instructed to provide her with a complete tray containing meat, potatoes, veggie, bread, fruit, and ice cream. She wouldn't touch anything as long as anyone else was in the room. Before she would even act interested, we had to pull curtains completely around her bed. I stood back and peeked through an opening between the curtains. The supervisor and I were guessing what she would eat first and if she would eat everything. I figured she would go for the ice cream, because it would be such a treat. The R.N. said mashed potatoes. We waited for some time to see what would happen. She kept fearfully looking around to make sure she was alone. Finally she grabbed the piece of bread and crammed it all into her mouth. We were so disappointed when she ate nothing else because she looked so famished. After a thorough exam the doctors discovered a weakened, very enlarged heart caused by long standing, untreated rheumatic fever. The police informed the parents where their little girl was. The father's arrival was explosive. He roared, yelled, swore and threatened us because we had his little girl without his permission. He had a good paying job at an airplane plant and tried to make excuses for the condition of his child. The police finally had to escort the parent away. This abused child's emotional and physical progress was very slow. The damage to her body was severe. I was moved on to my next special service without seeing the final result of this case. Child abuse and neglect are so sad.

Psychiatry

Last but not least, we found our way into psychiatry. Our instructors attempted to prepare us for this last great adventure into treating "diseases of the mind". We had many hours of classes learning about dementia, manic depression, and the four types of schizophrenia: simple, catatonic, hebephrenic, and paranoid. We incorporated new terms and words into our vocabulary. Psychoses, hysteria, hypochondriasis, compulsive behavior, hyperactivity, and hypoactivity plus many more were thrown at us daily. Before we were thrust into this "unknown darkness" we were taught, instructed, retaught, and drilled about caring for these poor unfortunate people. The "tough as nails" supervisor in this area repeatedly lectured us about treating each of these patients exactly as we had all our other patients. They were just ordinary folks with a mental problem which we were supposed to cure or at least alleviate. Just as we were reluctantly being pushed onto the "psychic" floor, almost as an after thought, she said, "Oh, yes, it's a good idea to keep yourself between the patient and the door while in their room." We didn't dare ask why, because we had been assured there were no dangerous people in our hospital. Oh, no.

Day one in the psychic unit arrived – our last special service before we could receive our black band on our caps. Of course, that would mean we were almost graduate nurses, so we were eager for the final hurdle. Soon we would understand why this was kept for the last phase to conquer. Several confidant young women entered the report room that morning. One of the toughest head nurses was in charge that morning. I wondered why so many head nurses and supervisors seemed so "hard". I wasn't sure I wanted to be one if I had to be so hard-hearted. Of course, most of them were very capable and perhaps were trying to hide a soft, caring heart. After report on all the patients, we were given our assigned patients to care for. With these final words from our head nurse, "Now remember, treat these people as you have all other patients in this hospital", we were on our way!

My first patient was a woman. After all these years, I can still close my eyes and bring back the image of this woman. What a vivid impression I have from this experience. Before I opened the door, I heard screams coming from within. That caused me to pause for just a moment. I remembered the words "these patients are just like all other sick ones". We had been given instructions to begin by taking temperature, pulse and respiration. We didn't want our mental patients to have physical ailments sneak up on us. So in spite of the screaming, I took a deep breath and entered the room. On that bed was an angry, wild-eyed woman who had both ankles and wrists restrained with leather restraints. There were long, stringy strands of gray hair hanging down over her face. She was screaming obscenities. I felt sorry for her and wondered if I released the restraints if she would feel better and become quiet. But I was much too afraid to do that because she was the wildest acting human I had ever seen. Instructions – take temps first. I got the thermometer, looked at this raving woman, and wondered just how I could take a temp. We learned long before that there were three ways to take temps – oral, axillary, and rectal. I could not imagine using any of the three on this lady, so I quickly exited to find the head nurse. Hearing my question brought aggravation and fury. I got yelled at in the room and outside of the room. She informed me that I had already been instructed to take all temps as elsewhere – orally. Again, I attempted to explain about my patient. Impatiently and loudly, I was ordered to get to work NOW!!!! I crept into the room again and confidently placed a thermometer under her tongue while she was screaming. Very promptly, she proceeded to chew the thermometer into tiny pieces. I could see her tongue bleeding. I wasn't as concerned about the small cuts on her tongue as I was the mercury in the thermometer. Where was it? Would it poison and kill her? Had I just killed my first patient? Once again, I ran for the head nurse. This time she came charging into the room, cleaned the woman's mouth without getting bit, and ordered me to feed the woman her breakfast. Old "NAILS" never even acted worried or concerned about the danger of mercury. It had the same effect on the patient – nothing. She didn't seem to even know her tongue and mouth should be sore. Whew! My first day on this unit was finally over with me wondering if I really wanted to be a nurse.

Memories of patients and experiences in the psychiatric unit remain more vivid and numerous for me. We often thought of one nurse who was sitting at the desk, engrossed in her charting at 3:15 a.m. She did not hear the male insomnious patient approach the desk from the rear and pick up a chart which was laying on the table. Using it as a weapon this "harmless" man proceeded to wallop the nurse on the head. Naturally, episodes like this did not really help us feel brave.

Since student nurses were supposed to help keep these people occupied in a constructive manner, a larger number were assigned to this floor. One morning, there were several of us doing our duty in this area. One of the over-active male patients suddenly and unexpectedly grabbed a fire extinguisher, activated it, began yelling that he was going to rape a nurse, and started pursuing terrified student nurses. Much to the chagrin of the hardened supervisor, we all fled in every direction possible – surprisingly fast! We all made it safely into a room where we could barricade the door, except Doris Carson. Poor Doris raced through a swinging door, which could be opened both ways. This harmless patient seemed content after thoroughly spraying Carson with the contents of the extinguisher. She was a basket case for quite some time. She was excused to go to the nurses' home to begin the clean-up process and regain her composure. She shampooed her hair numerous times before the sticky, gummy mess was removed. The rest of us were scolded, berated, reprimanded, and ridiculed for "making fools of ourselves" by running from someone who would do no harm. Our impatient supervisor wondered if we would ever learn. We didn't learn what she wanted us to. We all remained wary and somewhat fearful while serving in this department.

Many, many of the people we cared for in this department were extremely depressed and emotionally and spiritually disturbed. We heard one sentence over and over thousand of times from dozens of patients: "Why was I born, why was I ever born?" The common treatment of that day was electric shock and insulin shock therapy. Electrodes were fastened to the patient's head. It took at least six nurses to hold the patient in the bed when the current was turned on to prevent bodily harm to this poor individual. I hated every part of this procedure.

An interesting occurrence took place one morning when we were preparing a female patient for one of these treatments. Phyllis Bond was getting positioned to hold the patient's shoulders to prevent injury during the treatment. She inadvertently allowed her upper arm to be enticingly close and in line to the mouth of the woman. The inevitable happened. Those teeth sprung like a trap, catching Bond's upper inner arm with a vise-like grip. There was no release button to push. That woman had unbelievable strength and stamina. Bond didn't. She had much pain, some deep moans and a few tears, but was forced to remain very close to her patient. Finally, a Doctor gave a brief, mild anesthetic I.V. and blessed relief came for Bond. She was "battle-scarred" for quite some time. But each day, this group of determined young girls returned for more.

Insulin therapy was similar to electric shock treatments except it was done medically and over a longer period of time. Each morning the medicine nurse would go from patient to patient injecting doses of insulin. Each day the dosage was increased until it was a very large amount. Of course, the patients didn't need extra insulin in their bodies, so eventually they would go into insulin shock. It was the duty of the nurses to watch the patients closely and give previously prepared, rich, thick malts to offset the effects of the insulin. These people were soon back to "normal". The student nurse whose duty was to prepare the malts always managed to "overestimate" the amount needed. Of course, nothing should be wasted, so the students assigned to the area took care of the problem. Since most of us could rarely afford a treat, we happily enjoyed "licking the container clean". That was one of the few things we could enjoy in that area of nursing.

One of the important aspects of psychiatric treatment was group therapy. These patients were required to dress in their street clothes each day. Those who were not out of touch with reality were encouraged to enter into activities with other people who were able. One unforgettable, beautiful, pleasant day, I was given the assignment to take 8 or 10 patients who were really improving and responding well for a nice walk outdoors. Now I thought this would be a real treat. I would much rather be outside than in the hospital on such a nice day. We had this lovely area behind the hospital called Sleepy Hollow. That is where we planned to walk. I remember thinking, "Is this really nursing?" Things became very interesting. We had a very diverse group as you might imagine. In the group there was a petite, middle-aged lady who always wore a rust colored suit and a hat. Always a hat! She was super busy, energetic, over-active – always on the go, go, go. Then there was a man in his mid-thirties who was slow, slow, slow. He was phlegmatic, lethargic, and seemed to have no energy for anything. The teen-age boy was lots of fun; things were ho, ho, ho. He had a rather pleasant manner and was usually interesting to visit with. The rest of my group have been forgotten which is a good thing. If they would have made the lasting impression the other three people did, I may never have been a nurse. The walk began. Our busy lady in the hat took off like a rabbit –places to go and things to do. I called to her to stay with the group. She didn't hear me. The man had to meditate and concentrate a while before taking a step – each step. I tried to hurry him along just a little, to no avail. The rest of the group remained clustered around me like I imagined it would be. If I could only get Miss Busy-body and Mr. Slow Poke to stay with the well behaved patients! Then it happened! The teenager decided to climb this neat, inviting tree. He didn't want to come down. What should I do? Maybe I ought to run after the lady while I could still see her hat. Maybe I should hurry back to the man, grab him by the arm, and drag him along. I did not really consider climbing the tree. In all my dreams of being a nurse, this type of thing never entered my head. Was this really nursing? I began to wonder if I would ever get these people back into the hospital. If I did, I didn't want to ever get an assignment like this again. We got back. I was exhausted. I never had to do that again, so my nursing education continued.

Keeping psychiatric patients occupied was very important. As they improved in behavior, group activities were encouraged. They often played board games, checkers, and cards. The younger people really enjoyed this. One day there were four young men and women doing exceptionally well around a card table. They were certainly having fun playing dominoes. Upon observing this group everything seemed very normal. Suddenly, with no warning, one of the girls decided she could play much better in the nude. Quick as a cat she disrobed. It wasn't exactly the best therapy for the other patients. We had to move quickly to get everyone back to their own room. WOW! This helped teach us to forever be ready for the unexpected.

Many of the patients with "mental ailments" seemed to have deep spiritual needs. Numerous times we would hear about the need for forgiveness – not in those words, but with that meaning. Often these people would hear God speak to them. Instead of simply praying to God, they would seek unusual ways to contact Him. I remember one man who had a flashlight in his possession. The only way he felt he could contact God was by using his secret code. He would sit in a certain corner in his room and use the flashlight, turning it on and off with just the proper pauses and sequence. It always had to be pointed in the proper corner of the ceiling. He spent hours doing this. If he could have been treated by a trained minister, I'm sure the results would have been better.

Even the psychiatrists left memories with me. One of them had absolutely beautiful, perfect handwriting. He meticulously wrote out all his case histories. I thoroughly enjoyed reading every one of them. In 40 years I have never seen another doctor with such grand writing. He was a little stiff and formal in his actions, and not so interesting to be with. Not so with a more favorite doctor in this area.

He dressed informally and acted the same. He was always chewing a huge wad of bubble gum. He could smack, pop, and blow beautiful, big bubbles. He wasn't exactly professional in his demeanor. We rather enjoyed him, even though we often thought he appeared to need treatment himself. Many times, I wondered what his patients and their relatives thought of him.

Our final classes and this special service were completed at the same time. We were now within six months of graduation. If we passed our last final exam, we would be rewarded with a black band on our caps. This meant so very much to us. Now everyone would know at a glance that we were almost equal to an R.N. All other student nurses would look up to us and would honor us by asking advice of us. Ah, it was a good feeling. The final six months of our training was to be used to practice what we had learned, and to prepare us to "take charge". We needed it.

The black-banding ceremony was formal and quite impressive. Friends and family were invited. It was a candlelight program with the nursing school administrator in charge. She was extremely professional and tried to instill this in all her students. At this stage of our training, our class number had shrunk from 50 to 27. The hard work, difficulties, trials, discouragements, and tragic experiences had taken their toll. But the determination and enthusiasm of these remaining young women was unmatched. We still wanted to be the best nurses in the world and sometimes were cocky enough to actually feel we were the best. Alas, we still had much to learn.

In 2 ½ years, we had lived together, worked together, and played together. The bonds that drew us together had gradually strengthened over the months. We were more than friends, more than fellow nurses; we were more like a close-knit family. Sharing life and death situations and deeply emotional experiences creates a bond found nowhere else.

Cheap Fun

Most of us had very little money. No one had a car, but we found ways to have fun.

Doris Gibson had a high school friend who taught school at Sawyer. That happened to be where my sister Marge taught school. We thought it would be great fun to go see them when we had a day off. But how? Jackie Wight had a boyfriend who lived in Wichita, and he owned a car. She sweet-talked him into allowing her to drive a carload of student nurses to Sawyer. We weren't accustomed to such privileges. We were actually riding in a car, heading down a highway, leaving the hospital cares and concerns behind. What joy! We arrived safely and had a grand time visiting with loved ones. Of course, we knew we had to be back and behind those locked doors by 10:00 p.m. or we would be in very serious trouble. So the return trip began in plenty of time – we thought. Alas, we did not anticipate trouble. We had no idea what was causing that borrowed car to make such a peculiar noise in the motor. It got louder and louder and really began knocking. We decided it was serious, a little like a death rattle in an elderly patient with pneumonia. Jackie decided to ease it along until we reached a service station. That may have been a bad decision for the car, for Jackie, and for her relationship with Walt. I guess it is hard on motors to keep going with little or no oil. The attendant where we stopped assured us we would go no farther in that car. Panic button! We pushed it. We

38

absolutely could not be late. Should we call the housemother? We knew no one who could come rescue us. It was much too far to walk. As we were anxiously discussing our plight, we were completely unaware of the people who were listening in on our conversation. Soon a man approached us, asking about our grave concerns. We had to repeat several times the fact we were student nurses and had a curfew to meet. Our desperation must have impressed him. He became sympathetic when we convinced him how very strict the nursing school rules were. He kindly offered to take us straight to Wesley Nurses' Home if we could all get in the car. Of course, that was no problem. We were so thankful to get back safely and on time. Jackie had the next big problem. How was she going to tell Walt that his car was miles away and perhaps ruined? None of us got in on that conversation, but it must have gone well because after graduation, Jackie and Walt were married and became the parents of four sons.

Entertainment and fun became a challenge with very little money for that purpose. Most of the other things we did ended with less costly results. On July 4th, Wichita had a spectacular fireworks display down by the river. Of course, we didn't get to go, but we found a great way to get a good view. After getting tips from recent graduates, we followed their suggestions and instructions to get on the roof of the Huston Nurses' Home. This brick structure was four stories high and gave us an unobstructed view of the fireworks. Of course, this was also against the rules. Apparently, no person with authority found out because we were never reprimanded, grounded, or expelled.

Rough and tumble sports were cheap and a good way to vent our feelings and emotions. Our favorites were football, with very lax rules, and softball, with real rules.

Almost all the student nurses had special boyfriends. These devoted, patient guys would "rescue" us from our strict environment when we had a day or weekend off. Looking forward to those days or evenings out certainly helped us through some tough times.

Another source of fun was certain types of group activity. Prior to entering Wesley School of Nursing, I had learned of an entertaining way to "hypnotize" someone. Of course it was purely a trick. I shared the secret with a very few, carefully selected friends. My roommate was especially good at being "hypnotized". She carried out suggestions and instructions to the extreme. We would gather in one room and close the door. Then the cooperative "victim" was escorted from the room and down the hall out of hearing range. A simple activity such as singing, clapping, laughing, or crawling was selected by the group and the willing student returned to the room. As she sat in a chair with eyes closed, the "hypnotist" stood behind her. It was stressed how very important it was for everyone to completely concentrate on the chosen activity. The two people in the "act" really did have to concentrate. The "hypnotist" slowly rubbed the forehead and face of the seated friend. By using prearranged signals, the word was spelled out. Then the superior acting began. The spectators were almost always startled but delighted with the results. One evening we were enjoying a bit of this light hearted fun after a grueling day of heavy scientific studying. The activity came to a sudden, unexpected halt. You see, the "hypnotized" person always kept her eyes closed. This night she was instructed to crawl. After she received her instructions, she immediately plopped on the floor and began to crawl. Because the room was so crowded with spectators, one of them was helpful and opened the door. With head down, and with great speed, Thelma started down the hall on all fours. No one dreamed the housemother would be coming down the hall at that hour. It was hard to tell who was most surprised, Thelma or Mother

Maurer. Almost everyone else thought it was hilarious. I was a little fearful because I was the instigator of the whole ruse. At first Mother Maurer thought the stress of the nursing program had gotten to Thelma. We had to tell her it was all a joke and our method of having some inexpensive fun. I had to even explain fully and give our secret away. So much for that form of recreation. Mother Maurer was a good sport and seemed to thoroughly enjoy the plot. She often called me the probie with hocus-pocus insight.

Unusual Patients and Treatments

During my three years at Wesley Hospital I had many varied experiences. Medical procedures and treatments have changed drastically since the late 1940s. Many methods and equipment once used are now obsolete. How thankful I am for the improvements which have been made.

In those days, polio was one of the most feared and dreaded of all diseases. People who were stricken with bulbar polio were rendered incapable of breathing on their own. The only way to keep these people alive was to place them in an iron lung. It was a real nursing challenge to care for a person in an iron lung. I did this only once, which was enough to last a lifetime. The machine was a massive contraption which looked a little like a giant steel capsule. It opened at the head. The paralyzed patient was placed into the enclosed tube, with the head remaining out. An electric motor helped the chest to move up and down and the lungs to function as they should. The motor made lots of noise. I wondered how the poor patient could possibly endure the helplessness, the noise of the lung, and the complete dependence on someone else. If the person showed any improvement, they would be removed from their iron "prison" for as long as they could tolerate it. It was difficult to perform necessary nursing procedures while the patient was in the iron lung. It took great nursing skill and much patience when working in this area. How thankful I am for polio vaccine and respirators.

I worked briefly with another iron machine, but I cannot recall the name of it. The physician in this case was treating a woman for an unusual, stubborn disease. He had us place the woman in this machine. When it was activated, it would cause her body temperature to rise. I guess the elevated temperature was supposed to combat the illness. In this case it was my duty to keep constant check on the temperature of the lady. Of course we could not allow it to get too high or it could be fatal. When the temp reached a certain level, we would remove the patient. Back and forth and in and out. It was interesting but demanded utmost attention.

There are some diseases and conditions that are extremely unusual and rare. One of these, pseudocyesis, I got to see one time. I have never heard of a case since. This is really a false pregnancy. The woman's menses ceased and her abdomen gradually enlarged. All other signs of pregnancy were present. Of course, at that time, sonograms were unheard of. This patient had gone almost nine months convinced in her mind that she was going to become a mother. Hearing no fetal heart tones, the doctor considered other reasons for the symptoms. He administered a brief anesthetic and the enlargement of the abdomen disappeared. This was very traumatic and disturbing to the woman who wanted a baby quite badly.

One interesting experience I had at Wesley taught me a valuable lesson. A young, neat, attractive woman went to her doctor because of frequently recurring "crawling" sensations in her throat. His examination revealed nothing. He reassured her and sent her home. After some time she returned, pleading for help to relieve the crawly feeling in her throat. Again he checked her thoroughly, finding nothing to cause her trouble. She soon returned for the third time with the same complaint, this time showing much distress. The doctor ordered a barium swallow. She drank barium and many x-rays were taken, showing nothing. Continuing complaints resulted in another examination. A tube with a light on the end was passed into her tummy. The doctor looked around real well – nothing. By this time, the woman was frantic. She felt she had reached the end of the line. By this time the doctor was convinced this lady was mentally ill. He sent her to a psychiatrist and she was placed in the hospital for treatment of her psychosis. After some time spent there and much pacing of the halls, she continued to suffer from the same sensation. One afternoon when things were especially severe, she reached her finger down her throat and pulled out a long, long roundworm. RELIEF! She was cured. The reason the examinations failed to show the problem was because the worm would retreat into the upper intestine only to return into the throat when trying to escape. In most cases following this experience, I believed the patient no matter how weird the symptoms.

Unforgettable Patients

Several people I cared for while a student nurse remain tucked back in my memory. Some of them I barely met, others I cared for day after day and we got well acquainted. One female patient I did not get to know at all, but I remember the reason for her admission into our hospital. She had a three-year-old daughter who darted into the street into the path of a speeding vehicle. The mother ran into the street, grabbed her little girl and only had time to hurl her to the sidewalk. The little girl was unharmed, but the car struck the mother with great force. She sustained severe injuries, the most serious being brain damage. The area of the brain which received the irreparable injury was the temperature control area. Thermometers could not register the temperature because it got so high. Of course this mother died not knowing she had saved her child's life.

A middle-aged Greek lady had major abdominal surgery. The surgeon was the one who ordered me out of surgery for contaminating the surgical field. Of course, by now I had finished my time in surgery and was caring for post-op patients. This lady was rather plump and had a pleasant manner. I immediately knew I would enjoy caring for her. Present day surgical techniques and follow-up care have improved and changed dramatically. At that time, quite often, postoperative days were very uncomfortable for the patient. On the third day following her operation, this sweet lady was suffering terrible gas pains. I was working the 3 to 11 shift and spent much time in her room trying to make her comfortable. I finally got permission to do a procedure which I thought might help, even though it was unpleasant at the time. Ah, blessed relief! She was forever grateful and couldn't thank me enough. I was still in her room when the egotistical doctor breezed in to visit her. Since he had given the order for the treatment that I had given, he expected thanks and a show of appreciation from her. Instead, all she could do was bubble her praises for the "little student nurse", me. She continued to tell him I had saved her life. This lady was a very talkative person and couldn't seem to finish telling the good doctor how the nurse saved her life. He looked at me and his facial expression let us both know he did not agree with the thankful Greek woman. I wondered if he remembered me as well as I remembered him from those days in surgery. After recovery was complete this patient went home. It was then she proved she was sincerely thankful, because I received the largest box of expensive nuts I have ever seen. I shared them with all third floor nurses in Huston Nurses' Home.

Another encounter with this surgeon occurred when I was working on the surgical ward on the evening shift. This time the cranky, egotistical physician was the patient. He had undergone rectal surgery. The type of surgery he had was dreaded, painful, and very uncomfortable. I began this case with great trepidation, wondering if I would survive the ordeal. A great surprise awaited me. This doctor who had cursed and yelled at me and seemed to hate me was one of the nicest, most patient, and appreciative persons I cared for. Reversed roles did wonders for him. I had a little more respect for him after that.

Some people have been born with abnormalities that are quite noticeable and evident. One woman was unaware of her body anomaly until an unusual event occurred. She became pregnant and in nine months delivered a normal, full-term infant. Two months later she gave birth to another normal, full-term baby. She was born with two uteri. She conceived and two months later conceived again in the second uterus. We were fascinated. She was busy.

Nurses and Difficult M.D.s

Doctors and nurses are like most other people. Personalities vary, but sometimes seem more exaggerated. Since the work place of these medical professionals is at times quite stressful, personality flaws are much more noticeable. We student nurses soon discovered that there were some physicians who were always sweet, kind, gentle, and patient – even with inexperienced students. Then there were real bearcats who were often angry, short-tempered, and demanding. Some enjoyed scolding, belittling, and ridiculing young girls who thought they wanted to become nurses. On the other hand, the reactions of nurses were quite different. Some would practically kneel, bow down, and NEVER talk back. I was more timid than some, so I really admired those who stood up to these mighty men of medicine. (There were few female physicians at Wesley during our years of training.)

Most of the surgeons who kept the operating rooms busy owned their own instruments. After each operation, a nurse would clean the instruments prior to sterilization for the next use. If the surgery was to be done at Wesley, they would be taken directly to the sterilizing room. Occasionally, the doctor did surgery in other hospitals. Then he would take the instruments with him. The surgical suite at Wesley was on the fifth floor. One fine morning, a surgical procedure had just been completed. Angry, obscene words had been pouring from this doctor's mouth

48

throughout the operation. The nurses were disgusted and fed up with his antics. He remained in a bad mood. The stage was set. The instrument nurse asked, "What do you want me to do with your instruments?" His quick, testy reply was "I don't care, just throw them out the window." She promptly marched over to the window, opened it, and tossed them out. Surgical instruments are expensive and some are delicate. There were smiles of satisfaction on several faces and a scowl on one face. I did not see this occurrence but enjoyed hearing the details.

Dr. E was an older surgeon at the time we were in training. He had a very large practice, even though we considered him old-fashioned with some obsolete methods and ideas. Much of fourth floor was filled with his patients. He faithfully made rounds every morning to visit each patient. His entrance into the area was in a rather grand fashion. It was somewhat like a king or general accompanied by "all the king's men". A small troop of interns followed on his heels, heeding his every word and obeying every command. His "top sergeant" was a stout, obese, registered nurse who watched over him like a bulldog. She barked out most of the orders because she was in tune with his very thoughts. They were a real team. By the way, she loved sweets. Any time some kind patient gave the nurses a box of chocolates, she freely helped herself to not just one, but several, tasty pieces of candy. She considered herself to be several steps above all other R.N.s. And students were just scum that she had to endure. As you might imagine, the staff nurses had some difficulty tolerating this woman. The routine order which I think she loved to bark out was castor oil for every surgical patient on their third day following surgery. Horrible! It was nearly enough to kill a person. We wondered how he kept such a huge practice. Of course, it was the nurses who had to pull the poor patients through this awful experience. Quite often, it was also hard on the nurses. One fine morning, an appreciative patient gave the nurses a large box of chocolate covered cherries. Elaborate preparations were made prior to the grand entry. One of my classmates took a syringe and a large bored needle and very carefully removed most of the gooey, sweet innards of several chocolates. Just as carefully, she injected the popular castor oil into the center of the chocolate. It was truly a work of art. There was no visible sign of disturbance or "forced entry". By the time the entourage arrived at the nursing station, the choice candy was a welcome sight for our bossy R.N. She immediately grabbed a handful and began devouring them. She soon paused and asked the innocent students if they thought the candy tasted funny. Of course, they each slowly started to chew on an unadulterated chocolate. Everyone thought they tasted especially good. It was difficult to keep giant grins off faces as she finished all her selected candy. This special assistant of Dr. E was unable to complete her duties in surgery that morning. We all hoped these two people could experience the utter discomfort they routinely caused our post-operative patients. Forty-five years later several of our classmates had a reunion and once again enjoyed a hearty laugh together as we recalled the prank.

Barbara Sherwood was my dear classmate who lived next door. She was attractive, with dark hair and expressive, dark eyes. Her boundless energy was probably responsible for her slender figure. It was a pleasure to be with her because of her pleasant personality. We were all still trying to get accustomed to some of the cantankerous physicians. Barbara was asked to make rounds with one such doctor. All was going well as they worked their way down the hall. When they reached the far end, he decided to examine the patient and asked for a flashlight which Bobbie immediately produced. Ah, she was so proud to be

50

prepared. But trouble awaited. The batteries were weak and the light was quite dim. It was astounding how much this upset the impatient doctor. If you have never heard an angry physician how fortunate you are. He tore into Bobbie, yelling and swearing. He couldn't begin to see with such a poor flashlight. He continued raving, telling her to get a candle, he could probably see better. My, he was sarcastic. Bobbie seemed unperturbed as she sashayed up the hall to the nurse's station. She picked up an always available candle, lit it, and began the return trip to join the good doc. She walked slowly, elegantly, swishing her skirt, carrying the lighted candle. She must have felt like Florence Nightingale herself! Like a Queen, she entered the room, informing the doctor she had his candle. As the light flickered, Barbara remained serious. The patient was delighted. I think the doctor even had a slight smile. Bobbie scored one for the students that day. Hooray!

It seems many interns, residents, and some full-fledged doctors had the idea they were real Romeos. They seemed to think they were doing the young student nurses a big favor by "offering their services" to keep these poor girls from getting homesick. We had been warned about some of the persistent ones. One of the surgeons had fathered a daughter who definitely resembled him. The mother was now an R.N. The surgery nurses told us to beware, we might become pregnant just by standing across the operating table from him. I guess you could call him sexy.

One night I had to telephone a physician because one of his patients had developed some serious problems. It was bad timing. He promptly told me exactly what he was doing, in much greater detail than I wanted to hear. I was surprised, maybe shocked, and said, "Well, DOCTOR"!!! He laughed heartily and again detailed what I had interrupted. I wanted to hang up, but my patient needed help.

Progress

Things have changed drastically in the medical field since the 1940s and 1950s. When we first began working with real people in the hospital, there was no air conditioning. Wow, would it get hot when we were hurrying and working hard in the good old summertime. When we got off duty, we would hurry to the nurse's home, take a cool shower, and try to relax in our hot rooms. I guess it wasn't too bad. At least we survived.

Another interesting "lack" was no ballpoint pens. Yes, we used pen and ink. We had to distinguish between each shift when we charted, so different color ink was used. Black or blue ink was used on the 7 to 3 shift. The 3 to 11 shift got to use green ink. Red was reserved for the night crew. There were inkwells at each charting station. I can remember how we added beauty to our surroundings each spring. There were many spirea bushes at the nurses' home. We discovered if we placed sprigs of spirea in the different colored ink, the white blossoms would drink up the ink and the blossoms would change into pretty colors. We enjoyed the variety.

A real challenge came when much needed electricity was interrupted. We had no back-up systems. A few flashlights were available and we always had numerous, reliable candles. There were a few battery-powered lamps on stand-by in surgery in the event an operation or several operations were in progress. Probably the greatest challenge was the electrically powered iron lungs. They had to be operated by hand, which was no easy task. When a person's life is at stake, you can ignore weariness and tired muscles for a time.

In these more modern days, most hospital and medical equipment for routine patient care is disposable. When we were in training, it was a different story. Colon tubes, enema buckets, urinary catheters, syringes, and needles were all cleaned and sterilized for use on other patients. One boring assignment we had was a week or so in central supply where we would sharpen needles, clean all this equipment, and sterilize it for further use. The use of disposable supplies and equipment is certainly better for infection control and also frees nurses for more important and useful tasks. Ah, progress!

Another similar improvement was eradicating the need for a formula room. As mentioned before, all student nurses had to spend one week preparing formulas for hundred of feedings of newborns. Talk about boring! We were usually alone, mixing huge amounts of formula, pouring it into bottles and sterilizing them in a small, but powerful, autoclave. We always thought the hospital was using student nurses for free labor so they would not have to hire a person to mix formulas. Of course, they would fill us with these fearful stories about how some poor fool made this horrible mistake and put salt in the mixture instead of sugar. Naturally, it killed many babies. We felt sure this was their method of impressing upon our minds the necessity of careful preparation of formulas. Now all formula comes directly from the company ready for use. It even has a long shelf life. Oh, how we welcome progress.

Many nursing procedures have been improved dramatically or have even become obsolete. Hypodermoclysis. Modern nurses have probably never done this, or perhaps even heard of it. When infants or small children were quite ill or dehydrated, this method was used for treatment. A large bore needle was placed just under the skin of each anterior thigh and fluids were slowly dripped into the tissue. The legs would fill with fluid and become very swollen and tight. The body would then slowly absorb the needed liquid into the entire body. Now doctors have realized that even babies have veins that can carry fluids.

Oxygen tanks! Patients need oxygen. Years ago, we were required to move those huge, heavy tanks from their storage area to the patient room. With all our strength and muscle, we placed them on a dolly and rolled them into the patient room. Of course, we then had to move them off the dolly, place tubing on the gauge, and finally supply our patient with the necessary oxygen. Oh, yes, we then had to watch closely and move a new tank into the room to be available when the first one became empty. What a wonderful improvement when the oxygen was piped into each room in the hospital.

Glass drinking tubes – what a help for bedfast patients! They were even made with a nice bend in them so people could sip water while lying flat in bed. Maybe they were occasionally used as a weapon by confused or psychotic patients, but, as a whole, they were appreciated. Plastic, disposable straws – oh, so much better. Progress!

These are only a few of the modern conveniences which make nursing easier, safer, and more pleasant for everyone.

Our instructors worked very hard to turn young, inexperienced students into efficient, competent, caring, nurses who were not expected to make mistakes. We were told of at least two things that were absolutely unacceptable. One was to allow a woman to have a baby in bed, in the hall, in the bathroom, or anywhere without the physician present. The other was to find one of our patients dead. I often wondered just how this was to be avoided. I was soon to find out it wasn't.

I was working one of my first series of night duty as a student. I felt secure since I had such a good and experienced supervisor in charge of the floor. All the halls and patient rooms were kept rather dark, much darker than they are today. Flashlights were an absolute necessity when making rounds or answering lights. This night was quiet and uneventful. The floor supervisor was busy with her paperwork. A call light came on clear at the end of the hall where the large, eight bed, men's ward was located. I didn't like to answer lights in that ward at night because it was so dark, and it was difficult to tell who needed a nurse. Occasionally there were curtains pulled around the beds to allow privacy. I was using my flashlight beam to work my way from bed to bed in search of the man who had called for a nurse. Finally a man called to me and said, "I wish you would check on that man in the next bed. A while ago, he made some strange noises, then got quiet and wouldn't answer me." Sure enough, I found this man who had just come in for tests, who wasn't breathing. I could feel no pulse. This was my first experience with death and this was one of our no-nos. My heart started pounding as I hurried up that long, long hall to report to my head nurse. I rushed up to the desk and bluntly said, "I think Mr. C. in the ward is dead." She leaped up, dropped her pen, and cried out, "WHAT?" That was followed by bunch of "Oh, No's". You see, he had just come into the hospital that evening for tests. He did not appear ill at all. Now she had to call the doctor and the family. I stood back and watched, realizing how much I had to learn. How was I to know at that time how many of those kinds of phone calls I would be required to make in the next 40 years?

We were taught how to recognize the important signs and symptoms of a seriously ill patient whose condition was deteriorating to the point of death. I thought I would know that rather easily. Wrong!!! One day I was working on a medical floor and had to get finished with my work so I would not be late for a one o'clock class. My last task of the morning was to feed dinner to a lethargic, drowsy appearing, middle-aged woman. I pulled the head of her bed up and began spooning food into her mouth. Then I had to instruct her to chew and swallow. I could see this was going to be a long process. She wouldn't talk to me or respond. I kept trying to cram food into her mouth because they told us she really needed nourishment. Chew. Swallow. Chew. Swallow. When her head fell over to one side, I saw she had her cheek packed with food. When I finally called the head R.N. in, I felt terribly embarrassed and very ashamed of myself. All she said was "this patient is dying". Checking a patient's color is one of the most important signs of impending death. This woman was a very black, African American lady. I still feel shame, but think I would have done better had she been a white woman.

The girls in our class were all young. We had entered nursing school to help people, to play an important role in curing ills, easing pain, and restoring health. Death. We didn't even want to think about that. We thought of death as our enemy and connected it with failure. Of course, maturity and experience changed our beliefs on that subject. But at that stage in our lives we were not really prepared for the raw emotions that so often accompany the death of a favorite patient. One of these favorite patients was a very friendly, personable man, just the age of my Dad. Everyone could tell that he liked me and we had a special relationship. Student nurses were required to wear nametags with MISS and our last name. This man's wife was named Bridget. My nametag read Bridgeman. He immediately began calling me Bridget. I didn't care, but just hoped my instructor did not hear it. After some time in the hospital, long enough for us to become good friends, he was finally recovering and was nearly ready to go home. It was lunchtime and I had rolled the head of the bed up and placed the tray on the overbed table. He had just finished his meal when I went in to remove the tray. With no warning and without a sound, he just slumped over and died. My favorite patient was dead! The head nurse told me she would call the physician and the family but I was to take over when they arrived. AND HOW! I closed the door and tried to prepare myself, but I didn't know for what to prepare. I had not even been alone in a room with a dead person before. I put the head of the bed down and fixed everything as nice as possible. Soon, too soon for me, the family arrived. His wife came in and loudly cried out his name over and over as she wept bitterly. His sister rushed over to the bed, fell across his body, weeping and wailing. The sixteen-year-old daughter was the last to enter the room. She stopped at the closed door, her eyes huge and filled with horror. She quietly whispered, "Oh, daddy, oh, daddy, no no no". Then she leaned against the door and slowly slid to the floor. I might have seen something like this in the movies, but I had never been right in the midst of such an expression of emotion. I just stood there and cried with everyone else.

The head nurse came to my rescue (if you could call it that). She escorted me out of the room and gave me a lecture I never forgot. We were never to allow ourselves to become emotionally attached to a patient. We were NOT to cry. We had to be strong so we could be a source of strength and comfort to the patient's loved ones. Gradually, I was learning. In my years of nursing at our rural hospital, I discovered it was okay to cry when a patient died. Occasionally, the doctors did the same thing. Of course, we could still be strong for the family. Weeping seemed to show we really cared.

Approaching the Goal

After months and months of serious studying followed by weeks and weeks of putting into practice what we were learning, we were about to reach our goal of becoming full-fledged nurses. Throughout this whole process, we found ourselves drawn closely together. I really believe nothing else in life can bind hearts and lives so tightly as three years of nurses training. We lived together, experiencing the best and the worst in people and each other. We shared happy times and sad times. We encouraged each other during difficult trials. Shedding tears together helped us get through our most trying experiences. One important thing we learned was how vital a good sense of humor is. Nurses can and do laugh at things other people see no humor in. We can convey our feelings and thoughts with only a certain look. This is especially convenient in the presence of certain physicians. We soon discovered that nothing relieves tension like a good, hearty laugh. Sometimes laughing might seem inappropriate, but nurses understand and enjoy a delightful belly laugh.

Our instructors continued to watch over us but gradually gave us more responsibility. They wanted us to be fully prepared to be dependable, capable, responsible nurses. Until the day of our graduation, they were there for us. They didn't want anyone to fail the State Board exams. That would be a black mark on their record as well as ours.

State Board examination day finally arrived. We had to go to Emporia State College for our big two-day test. As was mentioned before, no one had a car, so transportation was by bus. Some of us third-floor girls thought we would rather go by car. So Phyllis Bond asked her boyfriend, Cleo, if we could use his old jalopy. Since he wanted to marry her as quickly as she graduated, he couldn't refuse. We six friends thought we were pretty special since we could go by auto at our own speed. We spent the nights in the college dormitory. After the first day of grueling exams we felt wiped out, and a little fearful of failure. Many of the girls from other nursing schools spent that night studying for the next day's tests. That thought never entered the heads of the Wesley students. We thought we were there for a good time. There happened to be a carnival in town at that time. So we went down to the fairgrounds, blew some precious money, rode the rides, and had ice cream. Wow, what fun. When we returned to the dorm, we found tense, nervous girls fretting over tomorrow's exams. After waiting months for the results, we felt the fun time at the carnival was good for us. Every person in our class passed State Boards.

Now the journey back to Wesley in Wichita would be carefree and fun. No worries. It was mid-summer and hot. We soon noticed Cleo's car was getting too hot. We needed to add water and knew we shouldn't wait. Since there was no service station available we decided to stop and carefully assess the situation. We really didn't want to ruin another boyfriend's car. Observant nurses that we were, how could we miss seeing the windmill, tank, and big herd of cows not too far out in a nearby pasture? A small soda bottle would work fine for carrying the needed water to the car. However, a large bull in the herd began eyeing us. Who was brave? Who was speedy? Hazel Brandt, who was one of the travelers, came from the Florence area. We were nearing her hometown and she thought she recognized these cattle. She assured us they were harmless. Crossing the tight, barbed wire fence was no easy task, but she finally accomplished it. The bull and cows were friendly, though curious. The thirsty car was eventually replenished with water and we were on our way. Hazel's kind mother had asked us to stop on our way back to Wesley, since they lived so close to the highway. What a pleasant stop that was. She had a beautiful, delicious, fried chicken dinner prepared for us. It was also much easier to get water there. Upon our return to Huston Nurses' Home, we were only too happy to relate our experiences to our bus-riding classmates.

Could it be possible that nurses training was almost completed? Graduation was just over a month away. All we had to do was work for dear old Wesley for free. Of course, we were still getting that wonderful experience.

It is always interesting to see how God works in our lives. Doors are oftentimes opened in unexpected ways which direct our paths. I started training in September. The following June a much smaller class began. There were two girls in this class from Sylvia, Patsy Hurst and Jane McElhaney. Patsy was like so many other student nurses and had a serious boyfriend who did not want to wait until graduation for marriage. She left school after two years to become Mrs. Lee Paulsen. I had almost forgotten about her. Shortly after we took State Board exams, I received a letter from a Dr. Longwood from Stafford. He wanted me to come and work in his office as soon as I graduated. Wow! How did he ever hear of me? I found out later it was Patsy who told him on one of her visits to his office as a patient. On my next day off, I went out for an interview and quickly told him I had not received the results of State Boards yet. I might not be an R.N. He wasn't worried about that. Since the hospital paid $200 a month for a six-day week and he paid $225 for 5 ½ days, I accepted his offer. It was especially nice since I would be getting married and living at Plevna, only 16 miles away.

For six months we had been black-banded seniors. Now we were actually preparing for graduation. Of course, our nursing school director made the major decisions about the speaker and program. Blue student uniforms with those stiff white collar and cuffs had been our working attire for 2 ½ years. Now we were instructed to select a white uniform to wear for graduation ceremonies. There was a very important stipulation: they had to all be exactly alike. Oh, yes, they were also to be long-sleeved, with turned-back cuffs requiring cuff links. The collar was to button up to the neck. Yes, we would certainly look professional when we crossed the stage to receive our long awaited diploma. Our director always looked sharp, neat, and professional. She wanted all her girls to look like that. After looking at pictures of several uniforms, then actually seeing some, we discovered a little problem. What looked really good on our two 5 foot, 10 inch girls didn't look that great on our 4 foot, 11 inch gal. I was very pleased with our selection and eventually wore out this uniform while working at Stafford.

Friday, September 1, 1950 was the date of our graduation. College Hill Methodist Church, which was several blocks south of the hospital, was the site for the big event. Proud parents, family and friends gathered for the occasion. There were numerous boyfriends in attendance who had waited impatiently for this night. There were also several weddings on the 2nd and 3rd of September. I cannot remember the speaker or what he said. Perhaps I was thinking of other things. I do remember two hymns that were sung. As I look back over the past 45 years, I appreciate the words and can understand why they were chosen.

I Would Be True

I would be true, for there are those who trust me;
I would be pure, for there are those who care;
I would be strong, for there is much to suffer,
I would be brave, for there is much to dare.

I would be friend of all the foe, the friendless;
I would be giving, and forget the gift;
I would be humble, for I know my weakness;
I would look up, and laugh, and love, and lift.

I would be prayerful through each busy moment;
I would be constantly in touch with God;
I would be tuned to hear His slightest whisper;
I would have faith to keep the path Christ trod.

A Charge to Keep

A charge to keep I have, a God to glorify;
A never dying soul to save, and fit it for the sky.

To serve the present age, My calling to fulfill;
O may it all my powers engage, to do my Masters will.
Arm me with jealous care, as in Thy sight to live,
And O, Thy servant, Lord, prepare, A strict account to give.

Help me to watch and pray, and on Thyself rely,
Assured, if I my trust betray, I shall forever die.

After the speaker, and special music by one of the doctors, we were each presented with our treasured diploma. Then we all stood on the stage together in our stiffly starched, look-alike uniforms and with our beloved white caps with the black band. In perfect unison, we united our voices in the Florence Nightingale Pledge, as we held a lighted candle.

I solemnly pledge myself before God and in the presence of this assembly, to pass my life in purity and to practice my profession faithfully. I will abstain from whatever is deleterious and mischievous, and will not take or knowingly administer any harmful drug. I will do all in my power to maintain and elevate the standard of my profession; and will hold in confidence all personal matters committed to my keeping and all family affairs coming to my knowledge in the practice of my calling. With loyalty will I endeavor to aid the physician in his work, and devote myself to the welfare of those committed to my care.

This pledge was first used in 1893, for a graduating class in the United States, but since has been used in many languages throughout the world. In more recent years, the use of this pledge has been discontinued. In fact, many new registered nurses have never heard of it. This saddens me. I would like to think that Florence Nightingale's lamp burns as brightly as ever as it continues to be passed down to dedicated nurses who are devoted to their profession.

Following the graduation ceremonies at the church, we all went back to Huston Nurses' Home for a reception. We all enjoyed visiting each other's families and meeting the future husbands who were there. What a happy, exciting time! Our long, difficult, but rewarding three years were over. Our goal had been reached. For so many months, we were so very eager and almost impatient to finish our training and move out of that place. We were ready to move on and up. For most of us, this meant marriage, and a career in our chosen profession. Suddenly the importance and significance of the moment hit us. It was time to bid farewell to our closest and dearest friends. We realized that, for some of us, our paths would never cross again. This was really good-bye. In that large, crowded room, we found ourselves pulling away from family and boyfriends and clustering together for the last time. Instead of joy and elation, we found our hearts were almost sad. We were not expecting this. As we stood there hugging, promising to try to keep in touch, and saying our final good-byes, someone suddenly began singing "Blest be the Tie that Binds". We all joined in as it became very quiet in that room. I still don't know who started the song, but I'm glad they did. The words to that song will always have a special meaning for me. I treasure the memory. Upon completion of the song, we returned to our families and special friends to depart from Huston Home, Wesley Hospital, and dear friends. An eventful, exciting, momentous chapter in my life was complete. Now on to new and greater things.

Nurse, Please!!

Book 2: The Life of a Nurse

Nurse, Please!!

Dr. Longwood and Office Nursing

Following marriage the day after graduation and taking on the duties of a housewife, I began work as an office nurse for Dr. Longwood at Stafford. A newly graduated nurse who successfully completed three strenuous years of nurse's training surely knows all that is necessary to be a good office nurse. Very soon I discovered there was much to learn.

How would I learn the necessary things to be a good office nurse? So many of the doctors I had worked with in Wichita had bad tempers and often cursed at the nurses. What could I expect of this doctor and father of three girls? I was thankful and relieved to discover how kind and patient this man was. I never heard him swear or use foul language. In fact, I cannot remember him even raising his voice. If he was upset or unhappy with a nurse's ineptness or mistake, he could be sarcastic, but always with a soft voice. Oh, how that could hurt! I learned much from him, some dealing with nursing procedures, but much more in dealing with human beings.

The office in which I began my duties as a graduate nurse was a nice brick building that included a waiting room and a small cubicle for the office girl (secretary, bookkeeper, bill collector, etc.). Of course the doctor had his private office. There were three examining rooms, one nearly twice the size of the others. This one was used for minor surgical procedures and laceration repairs plus more complicated diagnostic procedures. There was also a large treatment room, a small lab, an x-ray room and a drug room. Since there was no pharmacy in town, it was convenient for the patients to get their medications in the office rather than go to a neighboring city. One other R.N. was employed there. She was also trained to work in the lab and x-ray. She was a very accomplished surgical nurse and O.B. assistant. I was in awe of her.

Dr. Longwood was an excellent surgeon who worked under Dr. Hertzler of Halstead. Immediately after reporting for work, I found we had a complicated surgery scheduled. He wanted me to scrub in to assist along with Lucille. They told me to set up for the operation. Oh, my, it had been two years since I had done that. Did I remember? Did they want it like we did at Wesley? I was somewhat apprehensive as I began. I really wanted to get off on the right foot with my new job. I charged ahead, acting like I knew what I was doing. There was Lucille, watching like a hawk. Everything went smoothly throughout the surgery. Afterward I overheard Lucille tell the circulating nurse, "Boy, she sure knew how to set up an instrument table." I felt relief and happiness as I started a new aspect of nursing.

There was no job description then like we have today. I was just gradually eased into the daily routine. The office was closed on Tuesday and Saturday afternoons. Otherwise, the hours were 8 o'clock a.m. until 5 or 6 p.m. No appointments were made. The door would be locked at 5 o'clock, then he would see patients until the waiting room was empty. Wow, what a schedule! This doctor seemed to truly have a great desire to help people. My main duties at first were to assist with examinations, give injections, prepare medications, and assist with surgery and deliveries. Evening and nighttime births were the responsibility of

Lucille since she lived right across the street from the hospital. After a few weeks of satisfactory employment, I was expected to take histories and do some of the simple lab tests. Taking histories allowed me to become acquainted with some fine and wonderful people. I was becoming more confidant and was enjoying my newly developed knowledge. But there was much more to learn.

Nursing! Always be prepared for the unexpected. I learned this lesson rather abruptly one morning. I thought things were always quiet and routine in an office situation. Dr. and Lucille were making rounds at the hospital when the back door, which was to be used by office people only, suddenly burst open. A very distraught, hysterical mother ran in, screaming, "My baby, my baby, she's gone. Please help me." She plopped this small, limp, blue baby girl into my arms. My heart pounded. CPR was unknown at that time. I laid the infant on an examining table, frantically did all I knew to do, and started oxygen. I think God intervened because the child began to breathe and the color improved. It was not my expertise, but the mother thought I was a hero. A few years later, I worked with this child's grandmother at the hospital. She shared pictures of this girl who lived in another state at that time. We often recalled that incident.

One thing I immediately noticed about my doctor employer was that he seemed to truly care and enjoy all kinds of people. There was a very wealthy patient from St. John who often came into the office. This man always acted like he was much better than most of us common people. He was egotistical and barely had time to speak to this lowly nurse. One thing he thoroughly enjoyed was visiting with Dr. Longwood. On busy days, we dreaded seeing him come in, because it usually meant we would work overtime. He monopolized our doctor's time. Dr. always acted like he enjoyed the extra long visit. At first I

71

wondered if it was because this man had an elevated position in the society of a small town. But I soon noticed the overall–clad, humble man who came by often to pick up the large amount of trash and garbage from the clinic received the same treatment. He was uneducated, hard working, simple, and kindly. His wife did all the laundry for the office and you never saw cleaner, fresher linens. Oftentimes, Dr. would stop him at the back door for a good heart-to-heart visit. I began to notice how comfortable and relaxed he was while talking to this friendly but poor man. It was clearly evident that he could truly appreciate and enjoy people from all walks of life. This impressed me. I soon discovered that I needed to learn it for myself.

One afternoon a new patient came to the waiting room. The receptionist seemed awfully happy and relieved when I called her into an examining room - the smallest one we had, but the only open one. Of course, I closed the door so I could get a history in private. The patient was a young woman, one of the dirtiest creatures I had ever seen. Now, understand, this was not new, fresh dirt. This was an accumulation of filth and grime that had been present for weeks. She might not have known what a bath was. She apparently had had insufficient protection during her monthly periods. Her clothes were quite soiled and stained. The odor was overwhelming. The door to that tiny room was closed. I thought I might become sick. The complaints and symptoms all added up to the necessity of a full exam, including a pelvic. After finally exiting the room, I stuck my head out the back door for a quick refreshing breath of good, pure air. Then I gave my report to Dr. Longwood. He quietly said, "Let's go in and see what's wrong with her." When he said we should do the complete exam, I asked, "Oh, do we have to?" Very firmly, he said we would treat this woman just like we would any other person. She is a human being and will be treated like one. We will give her the same consideration, time and care we do anyone else. Wow! I learned a valuable lesson and felt like I had really been reprimanded. Then Dr. looked at me, smiled, and said that we should take a deep breath, enter quickly, do the exam, and head for fresh air. We did. After the patient left the clinic, we did not use that room the rest of the day. We closed that door and opened the window to share the odors with the great outdoors. It was amazing how long this woman's "calling card" remained with us.

Another thing I learned from Dr. Longwood was to try to remain calm (at least on the outside) no matter what the situation is. One day this big, raw-boned, German man came striding into the clinic after severing his arm. They both seemed calm. The nurse wasn't. They both acted like this was an every day occurrence. I also quickly noticed that every movement the doctor made accomplished something, served a purpose. There was no wasted movement either in surgery or when working an emergency. He appeared to never really hurry, but I found myself rushing just to keep up with his actions.

This physician exhibited compassion and tenderness without shame. Several times I watched him embrace relatives of dead or dying patients. This can sometimes be very difficult. A fine Christian man, only 21 years old, was admitted to the hospital for diagnosis of serious signs and symptoms. When all the exams and test results were completed, the dreaded diagnosis of leukemia was made. At that time there was no treatment available as we have today. It was like a death sentence. The doctor sat at the nurse's station a long time preparing himself for the task of breaking this news to the "boy". He agonized, even saying he would rather cut his own arm off than tell that young man he had only a few weeks to live. He cared so much and wasn't ashamed to show it.

Another comment by the doctor made an impression on me. There was a bad automobile accident. The driver of the car was quite drunk. His wife and mother of his little girl was killed. This might be a foolish thing for me to remember, but the woman's eyes remained open. I recall thinking she died so suddenly, she didn't even have time to shut her eyes. The distraught husband and father repeated over and over, "I'll never, never drive a car again." After returning to the office, Dr. Longwood said, "He should have said he would never ever take a drink again." Of course, this man drove a car again for years and years. He also drank in excess again. He also married again, twice.

In 1950 the practice of medicine was much different than it is today. There were only a few antibiotics, no CPR, no organ transplants, no CAT scans or MRIs, less sophisticated and fewer available laboratory procedures, and no Red Cross blood supply. The doctors depended much more on their own sense and knowledge, and their sense of sight, hearing, touch, and smell. The lack of a Red Cross blood supply was responsible for a great feeling of community spirit and cooperation. All the healthy and willing people in the entire area had their blood type taken, recorded on cards, and filed in each doctor's office. If a blood transfusion was needed, day or night, the person next in line with the correct type was called in for a direct, person-to-person transfusion. Small town people cared for one another and were so ready to give of themselves. No selling of blood here. Of course, now we know that cross matching is of great importance. And since AIDS reared its ugly head, this obsolete method would be unsafe.

In the spring of 1951, a very serious, complicated surgery was scheduled for one of Dr. Longwood's patients. He anticipated a lengthy, life threatening procedure. Wanting to be prepared and doing everything possible for the good of his patient, he called for three blood donors to

74

come in to be available, if blood was needed. The interesting thing was the patient had the rarest blood type – AB negative. About 15% of all people are type AB and about 15% of those are negative. Three people in the entire area had the desired and necessary type. And, of course, they also had a willing heart.

It was almost time for surgery. Both doctors were present and almost finished scrubbing. Both nurses were already scrubbed in and preparing instruments. The patient had not been brought into the operating room yet, when pandemonium erupted. I had never heard anyone call Dr. Longwood by his first name, Orlan, so I hardly knew what was happening when I heard that name being screamed over and over. There was terrible panic and commotion. A victim from an auto wreck was being brought into the surgery area. A boy from Hudson and his freshman sister were driving to school and rolled the car. The girl was thrown through the windshield, onto and through a barbed-wire fence. She had received horrible head and facial lacerations. She was immediately brought into the room prepared for the surgical patient. Lacerations of the head and forehead exposed the skull. A large cut went completely through the right cheek and her tongue was almost cut off. There was a horrific laceration on her neck, reaching from ear to ear. The jugular vein was entirely exposed. The cuts on her arms seemed inconsequential. After losing most of her blood, she appeared dead and was unresponsive. The woman who was scheduled for surgery was left in her patient room and all thought and effort was placed on the poor student from Hudson. A quick order was given to get her blood type. It was AB negative. Blood donors were there, ready and willing. Operating room, doctors, nurses, instruments were immediately available. The girl was brought in with no blood pressure, no color, extremely weak pulse, and very little blood. After three units of blood, and several hundred sutures, she had blood pressure, improved color and a much better pulse ... and LIFE. I have never seen so many things work out so perfectly. Everything was timed just exactly right. Was this all a coincidence? I hardly think so. I think we all felt God overseeing the whole episode. By the way, the surgery of the original patient was postponed until a new source of blood could be made available.

One of my duties as an office nurse was to give injections. I became well acquainted with people who needed weekly allergy shots. Other injections were necessary on a regular basis. Roger was a 4-year-old boy who had a rather serious ailment. Children do not appreciate getting "stuck". Poor Roger was no exception, and he needed shots about every four days. I always visited with him prior to even preparing the syringe, needle and medication. We became very good friends. It wasn't long before I was the only one he allowed to give him the shot. Soon, there were no tears. The next point in our progress was a little smile instead of tears following each injection. Ah, yes, we were truly friends. Even though I felt this close friendship, I was surprised when he asked if he could go home with me one Tuesday afternoon. (He knew we had that afternoon off.) He wanted me to take him fishing in the river in our pasture. He loved to fish. I knew nothing about fishing. Roger's mother was very pleased with the idea and planned to come get him after dark. I was a little uneasy about being responsible for a sickly boy, but agreed to the plan. He was so happy riding home with me. I borrowed an old bamboo fishing pole from my father-in-law and we headed for the pasture. I cannot remember if we caught a fish, probably not, but little Roger was very content and happy. He recovered from his illness, and became a healthy young man. He was so well that I didn't see him anymore. Through friends and family, I tried to follow his progress in life. He became a missionary and was far from the area for years. Recently, I heard he retired from the mission field and moved back to the Stafford community. I wonder if he would remember me and our fishing experience.

Working in Dr. Longwood's office was not all work and no fun. He treated his three female employees like we were members of his family. He had three daughters, two in high school, and one in grade school. His only son died when very young. The youngest girl was a victim of polio and was left with a weak leg and a decided limp. She was vivacious and intelligent. Dr. wanted her to have every chance to overcome her weakness. He put a swimming pool in his back yard and insisted she swim every day to strengthen her leg. She became an accomplished swimmer and nearly made the Olympic team, but of course, she kept her limp.

In the summertime when we were able to close the doors at noon, Dr. encouraged us three employees to make use of the pool for a refreshing swim. My, how we enjoyed that. He also invited us into his home for parties and holiday celebrations. His wife was always sweet and gracious. She made us so welcome.

I was now an R.N., but soon realized there were constantly more things to learn. Dr. Longwood was an excellent teacher. He allowed me to do things in surgery that only interns were doing in Wesley. I learned a lot in the operating room as well as in the delivery room.

One important thing I learned was completely separate from technical procedures. His care, concern, and commitment to every patient was so evident. He tried to accommodate each person, according to their time. We did things then that could not be done now. If someone needed a refill on medications (no drug store in town), and could not get to town during office hours, we simply left it wrapped and labeled in the doorway between the storm door and the locked inner door. Sometimes there were 4 or 5 packages at a time. The next morning they had all been picked up and by the right people. Other times he would ask Lucille or I to go to someone's home to give an injection – only if they had no transportation to the clinic. Several times I took medications to Sylvia or Plevna for one of his patients. One time he even asked me if I would transport a very poor, older woman to her home in Sylvia. Of course I did.

He also tried to adjust costs and fees to avoid hardships for people with little money. I remember one time, he spent time trying to figure accurately just how much the x-ray and lab solutions cost him. Then he charged only for that, nothing for his time or for an office call. No payment was ever received. I enjoyed teasing him about that.

There was a well-known business family in the area that frequented the office often, sometimes with insignificant complaints. They had a very comfortable life style and appeared affluent. They never paid their doctor bills. The wife needed surgery late one spring, and recovered rapidly. Later, a notice came to the office that insurance covering the entire cost of surgery had been paid – to the family. That summer the entire family enjoyed a lovely vacation in Colorado, apparently with insurance money. No payment was ever received by the doctor. Such is life. Dr. was disturbed and disappointed, but continued to care for the family.

Unwed mothers were much more rare then than they are now. There was also a certain feeling of shame and embarrassment. I remember three different cases of this type while I was employed there. The outcomes are varied and interesting. One mother brought her young high school girl in because of troublesome symptoms. The results of the examination showed the girl was pregnant. Very gently, the doctor informed them of his findings. The mother completely lost it and became hysterical. The girl remained absolutely stoic. A long period of time, advice, and discussion of the father of the unborn baby ensued. Marriage was the decision. This couple has now raised their nice family, and that first-born child is now serving the Lord in a special way.

One of the other cases was quite different. The young teen-age girl came in alone. Her mother had recently died and her father was abusive. He demanded much of her. She had difficulty coping. When she came in it was very difficult to obtain a history. She was quite withdrawn and reluctant to talk at all. The diagnosis of pregnancy was made and she also got married. It has been a trouble filled marriage and the product of that relationship has been nothing but huge problems.

The results of the third case were also tragic. This family came in from one of the towns west of Stafford. The mother brought the young daughter in to the clinic because she suspected the girl was pregnant. She was correct. This mother was especially kind, soft-spoken, and supportive. This couple did not get married, but the young man remained at her side throughout the pregnancy. He was with her when she came in for the birth of the baby. Of course the parents were there also. Labor and delivery went along smoothly without complications. Immediately following the birth of a fine beautiful baby, the mother went into convulsions and died. Feverish attempts at resuscitation failed. Oh, what a difficult, agonizing time followed. The doctor had to tell the father of the baby and the parents of the girl that this new mother was dead. The doctor, nurses, and loved ones all shed tears and shared their grief together. I have not had the opportunity to know the outcome of this case. I do know the grandmother raised the child. I have seen her once or twice since and saw her name in the newspaper once, but do not know what has happened to the child. This was the only maternal death I had to deal with after I left Wesley Hospital.

One couple who doctored with Dr. Longwood made an impression on me. They were strikingly good looking. He was dark and very handsome. She also had dark hair and was beautiful. She had a wonderful personality with a delightful sense of humor. I enjoyed their visits to the clinic. I soon learned that the husband was super sensitive to blood, pain (his or his wife's), and even hospital smells. At the birth of both of his children, he increased the workload of the nurses by fainting. Any time the children had even the slightest, most insignificant little accident, he promptly fainted. His wife became accustomed to it, fully expected it, and thought it was hilarious. One evening, they were in an accident, and the wife received a broken leg. He had no injuries, but she fully expected him to faint away. Instead, he reacted beautifully. Carefully, gently, and calmly, he got her to the hospital where they were met by the doctor. The moment the doctor got there to take over, the husband obliged by keeling over in a dead faint. I remember Dr. was a bit disgusted at this delayed reaction.

A young mother with two daughters came into the clinic after discovering a lump in her breast. Dr. felt certain, by the firmness and feel of the lump, that we were dealing with a malignancy. He was positive and felt it was seriously advanced. He wanted to do surgery immediately and not wait for a biopsy. She would not agree without laboratory verification. Of course, this could not be done at Stafford and it did take time. The report came back Saturday afternoon and was as he expected. He knew Lucille and I were habitual churchgoers. He asked if we would be willing to assist with surgery on Sunday morning, because he didn't want to wait another day. Of course, we agreed. An extensive radical mastectomy was performed.

Very little advances had been made in cancer treatments at that time. The important thing was early diagnosis and extensive surgery. He spent much time that morning trying to get all involved lymph nodes. He felt sad because he considered her prognosis poor. She recovered, raised her children, and lived a beautiful, productive life. In 1995, I visited with her while she was in the hospital for congestive heart failure. We recalled that Sunday morning back in 1951 and rejoiced together that she had been able to enjoy not only her grandchildren but some new great grandchildren as well. She died shortly after that. She had become a dear Christian friend of mine. When I went to the mortuary prior to her funeral, I recalled Dr. Longwood's concern about delaying surgery even one day. She enjoyed a full, long life and outlived the doctor.

Interesting non-medical problems took the doctor's time in the office. There was a wealthy couple from one of the neighboring towns that made rather regular office calls. Neither seemed to have serious medical problems. The man came in much more often than his wife. He was very egotistical and proud of his wealth, which, by the way, was not due to hard work on his part. He acted like we nurses should bow down to him when he entered the room. Arrogant! His wife was attractive and much more pleasant to be with. One night, completely unexpectedly, he had a massive heart attack and died. About two weeks following the funeral, his widow came into the office to see the doctor. She had a problem she wanted to discuss with her physician. You see, when completing the business with the mortician, he gallantly offered to come to her home and take care of any and all of her physical needs in the absence of a husband. She was shocked and disturbed, almost angry. She didn't know how to handle the situation. She didn't even want to meet this man on the street. The doctor spent a long time visiting with her and she left feeling much better. She soon moved away and I never saw her again.

Working in a doctor's office had many advantages. There were few real crises to deal with. We got well acquainted with many people; some were real characters. One sweet little old lady lived less than a block from the clinic and was an avid gardener. From springtime into the fall, she kept us supplied with a fresh bouquet of flowers to soften and beautify the "coldness" of a waiting room. A farm woman would often bring home-grown products from her garden for the doctor. One hard-working farm wife even brought freshly dressed chicken for her favorite physician. Kind people. One short, stout lady reported in one day with the concerned statement that she was hemorrhaging. We immediately took her to an examining room, only to find a minute spot of blood. Of course, she needed a check-up to find the cause, but her definition of hemorrhage was different from ours. Another woman, one of my favorites, was rushed in without stopping to register with the receptionist. She was canning beans when one of the jars broke. She received a severe laceration on her hand, severing an artery. I happened to be the available person to greet her. My first attempts at stopping the "gusher" type bleeding was futile. I grabbed a towel to try to keep the regular bursts of spraying blood from reaching all the walls and ceilings. I knew I would be expected to clean the mess. I finally got a tourniquet tight enough to quench the flow of blood. Dr. Longwood did a beautiful job suturing the deep cut. The patient wanted to return home and finish canning her beans. What a lady!

An elderly Irishman with a distinct brogue fascinated me. I enjoyed listening to him talk. He came in one day explaining how he happened to fall and receive such a tremendously huge bruise. He actually had a large hematoma, which is a collection of blood in the tissues which has formed a clot. Often these will take care of themselves by dissolving into the surrounding tissue. This one was much too large and remained sore and painful. He was taken to surgery so the area could be incised and drained. Since it was a minor procedure, I was the only nurse to assist the doctor. Everything was set up and ready. After a small, local anesthetic, Dr. took a scalpel and made an incision over the hematoma. There was so much pressure and free blood that it sprayed out with much force. I was right in the line of fire. It got me square in the face and down my uniform. Mr. M. laughed as only an Irishman could, and all those Irish words came rolling off his tongue. Oh, how he enjoyed it. The operation was put on pause until he could quit laughing and I could get cleaned up so I could at least see. The blood clot which was removed looked about the size of half a liver, but it did not faze him. After that, every time he saw me, he immediately began to laugh. We found one way to bring happiness to a patient.

Getting to know and become friends with patients was nice, but meeting other registered nurses was special in a different way. Lucille Bagley was the first one I met because she was the other office nurse in the clinic. She had been there several years and was well established in her hometown. She was intelligent, capable, self-assured, neat, nice looking, and a perfectionist. I was in awe of her. At first, I wasn't sure just how she felt about me entering her domain. It took a few weeks before she seemed to feel I was capable of doing the work in a satisfactory manner. Then we became good friends and enjoyed many good times together.

The first nurse I met at the hospital was Mona Rumford. She was the circulating nurse in surgery. She was quiet, soft-spoken, tenderhearted, and caring. She had a vast amount of experience. During World War II she served as an Army Nurse overseas. We rarely heard about her work during the war. Nursing wasn't her only field of expertise. She was also a registered x-ray technician and registered lab technician. I watched her assist the surgeon during major surgery. It seemed to me she could do anything and do it well. We became dear friends and several years later, after I became a mother, we got together socially with our husbands and another couple. What good times we had eating together in each other's homes and then having a lively game of pinochle.

Several nurses who were employed at the hospital were very interesting people. There were three older ones with unique personalities. I won't mention their names. The first one was a capable, calloused, cool charge nurse. Nothing seemed to bother her or surprise her. She had lost her middle finger on her right hand, but it didn't seem to hinder her activities in any way. She functioned like a machine, doing her job, showing little compassion.

The second one had become rather crusty and had an abrupt, brusque manner. She hated to care for children and it was very evident. After I became better acquainted with her, I sensed that she really cared for her patients, but wanted to show no emotion to indicate that. I think she felt insecure caring for little ones. I felt sorry for her. The nurses and other hospital employees exchanged names for our Christmas parties. One year she received a pair of dress hose. Everyone soon knew that she was not pleased. She let out a loud HARRUMPH and tossed them into the wastebasket. She had my name that year and I still have the gift she chose for me. It is a wall hanging – a plate with the Lord's Prayer on it.

The third one was an older, experienced nurse. She was a co-worker much longer. She was intelligent and well educated, but had little common sense. Cleanliness seemed unimportant to her – a trained nurse. Personal appearance was certainly not a plus for her. Her kindness and love for everyone was very evident. It was interesting to see her unusual way to awaken her patients in the early morning hours. Most patients would smile as they heard her come into their room singing a good morning song to them. When she worked the evening shift it might be a lullaby as she tucked them in. Often she did extra, unordered things to make people happy or comfortable. It didn't matter if she worked overtime with no pay; she enjoyed her work and her patients. One time she had just finished cleaning up an unfortunate adult who had had an "accident" in bed. She returned to the nurse's station with the telltale signs of brown stains on her hands. At that time she decided it was time for a snack and proceeded to cut an apple into quarters and eat it. The other nurse saw this action and was aghast. She yelled, "You haven't washed your hands." After looking at her brown stained hands, she nonchalantly replied, "Oh, I guess not." She ambled off to wash her hands. All the rest of us nurses were always quite eager to get to the utility room to scrub our hands with surgical soap and a brush. This was unimportant to this dear woman. I remember this unforgettable nurse because of a personal experience as her patient. I had just given birth to our third son and was back in my room resting. She detected a rather dramatic drop in my pulse and blood pressure which she immediately reported to the physician. A visit from the doctor and the prescribed medication was not quite enough for her. She was sure an eggnog would make me feel much better. She went two floors down to the kitchen and prepared one. I had never tasted one in my life and wasn't sure I wanted to. With her gentle urging I drank it. She was pleased. Later I wondered if her hands were clean when she prepared my special drink. If they were not clean, I guess it did no harm because I survived. These three nurses have passed on and gone to their rewards years ago. But memories of them, their actions and personalities, are tucked away in my brain.

Elizabeth was young and pretty, a new R.N. who was working the evening shift at the hospital when I was working in Dr. Longwood's office. I did not become well acquainted with her but certainly remember the tragedy that befell her. Her boyfriend was planning to pick her up at 11:00 when she finished her shift. He was late, which did not please her. The later he was, the more disturbed she became. She was almost angry, and decided to go on home. Just then an ambulance arrived bringing her special friend whom she planned to marry. He had wrecked his car 7 or 8 miles south of town. He had come up under the dashboard of the car, receiving severe lacerations in the elbow area of both arms. The arteries were severed and it looked like he had tried desperately to get out of the car. He bled to death. No other injuries were evident. Elizabeth was still at the hospital to greet the accident victim. What a devastating shock! She soon left Stafford to start a new life in other surroundings. I never heard from her again.

After working for Dr. Longwood for two years, I decided I wanted to quit and start a family. Since I had begun in September, I thought that would be a good month to tell Dr. I wanted to quit. I liked him so much and enjoyed the work so well that each time I started in to resign, I lost my nerve. After trying for two months, I finally informed him that I wanted to quit. Of course, I told him the reason. He didn't seem too surprised. I felt fortunate to have him deliver all four of our sons and sew up all the lacerations and even do surgery on the boys.

Stafford Hospital

After my stint as an office nurse, I really thought my nursing days were over. Now I would be a full time wife and mother. How wrong! Even with little babies or toddlers at home, calls would come for special-duty nurses. Hospitals were not equipped with intensive care units, so nurses were needed around the clock. We were never supposed to ask the type of patient or the cause for a much needed nurse. We were expected to be the ever willing, duty-bound, faithful servant. Two different times I refused, because of pressing family needs. I was made to feel very guilty. Both times the patient died and I was made to feel it was partially my fault. And one of the people was from Plevna.

I was still nursing one of my babies when the next call came. Because of that, I began to hesitate. The nurse who was calling said they could find no one else. She then pleaded her case. The patient was a mother who had just delivered a baby girl. Because of severe complications, the mother was about to die. I went. The new father met me at the door with much emotion and excessive expressions of thanksgiving. He would forever be indebted to me if I could only help save the life of his beloved wife. I don't think I ever put in a more tiring and difficult eight hours. Just as my eight hours were ending, the crises seemed to be subsiding. The new mother survived and soon took her little baby home. I presumed this appreciative husband and father would be only too happy to pay the special nurse who neglected her own baby to care for his wife. Wrong!!! As months passed and requests for payment went unanswered, I decided to give up and just accept for payment the satisfaction of knowing I had a small part in saving a life. It was then that I received my payment.

One afternoon I had a telephone call urging me to come quickly to the hospital. A 34-year-old woman had been stung by a wasp and was having a severe allergic reaction. They wanted more help. My ever present and willing mother-in-law was available and came to my house. I got ready in double time to respond to the call. The lady died before I had a chance to reach the hospital. She had had a milder reaction previously, so she knew she was in trouble. Progress in the medical field has given us first aid kits for those who are allergic to insect stings.

Special care nursing was not my favorite aspect of nursing. The call usually came with little warning and the patient was often critical. Many times it ended in death. Of course, now we have our critical care units. That answers the need much better.

Night Nurse

In 1958, I thought I was very busy with three little boys to care for. Of course, husbands take some time, too. Then a call came from a dear nurse friend of mine. She happened to be the hospital administrator and director of nurses. The regular night nurse, Bertha Thomas, was scheduled for necessary surgery and would be unable to work for six weeks. She asked in a rather pleading manner if I would consider working those few weeks until Bertha could return. At that time, full time meant 5 ½ nights a week. That meant five nights one week and six nights the next week. It sounded overwhelming to me. This necessitated a family conference. I really needed some time for sleep. My mother-in-law was willing. The boys were gung-ho because Grandma always had goodies and never scolded them. Daddy said okay since it was only for a short time. So began my adventure in night nursing and trying to sleep in the daytime. Little did I dream that it would go on and on until 1993. You see when Bertha returned, the next request came. Would I fill in on her nights off? That just meant one night one week and two the next. Piece of cake! It really wasn't too bad. I just tried to sleep through the noon hour once every two weeks. As weeks and months passed the request would come for another night or so a week. In a few years it was full time. They even decided full time would be forty hours.

89

At that time the hospital was an old two-story building with a full basement. The surgery and delivery rooms were on the second floor on the north end. Adjacent to them was the nursery. On the south end were patient rooms for the O.B. and surgical patients. There was a slow moving elevator and staircase in the center of the building. The first floor was used for medical patients and also housed the business office. The kitchen and laundry were in the basement. This old building was usually a very busy place. It was the birthplace for our three oldest sons. Kyle got to arrive in the much more modern hospital.

In some ways this old hospital building just seemed like a warm, comfortable, homey haven. In those days, drugs were no problem. I cannot remember a gunshot victim for a patient. We had the usual illnesses common at that time, numerous farm related accidents and lots of babies. The doors were never locked and we never felt any fear from the outside world. We did have some excitement from time to time. One dark, late spring night, the nurses investigated an interesting, familiar noise. The unusual thing was the area of the hospital in which the sound originated. Following the sound of a weak, little cry, a nurse opened the front door. What a shock for her to pick up a precious, newborn, baby girl wrapped in "swaddling clothes". The nurses made a quick call to one of the doctors and the director of nurses. The usual newborn care was done. The infant was warmed, bathed, dressed, and fed. The director of nurses was childless and wanted the baby for her own. She tried. The doctor tried to help her obtain custody of the deserted baby. Of course, the State had the legal right to place the infant in a home. The director of nurses did not get her wish to become a mother.

The education process of nursing never seems to stop. It is a constant, ongoing, learning experience. It was new to me to not have a night supervisor to turn to for advice or help. I was on my own. I tried to recall many of the important things learned in training. I soon found that many things are different in a rural setting. Benny was a young man who had very serious, unplanned surgery. The outcome was tragic. Everyone knew he would not survive. I vividly remembered my first experience with death as a young student nurse, how I was told it was the responsibility of the nurse to be strong for the family, with no weeping or spilling of tears. So I prepared myself when death was near. But I was in for another surprise. The director of nurses and doctor both came into the hospital. They both greeted the family with hugs and tears. No one was ashamed or embarrassed. The relatives seemed to expect it and appreciate it. I certainly felt more comfortable with this warm, friendly showing of emotion.

Farm Related Accidents

As a farmer's wife and mother, I was especially touched by the first farm accident patients I cared for. A four-year-old boy was enjoying a tractor ride with his grandfather. I never knew how it happened, but the lad fell off the tractor. The grandfather made a gallant effort to save the boy and ended up under the large wheel of the vehicle. In those days most doctors and hospitals cared for all types of patients. The little fellow had head injuries and a less serious injury to his chest. We cared for him in an oxygen tent. His head and face were quite swollen. His eyes had the appearance of a frog. It was a long ordeal, but he survived. The grandpa suffered with much more critical injuries. I think most of his bones must have been broken. He was a very kind and gentle man. He lived three days, long enough to be assured the precious boy would probably survive the traumatic ordeal and only because of his heroic efforts which resulted in his own death.

Little boys seem fascinated with tractors, trucks, and big farm equipment. This accident happened many years later when the machinery was bigger and more powerful. This boy was probably 8 or 9-years-old when he fell from a tractor and was run over with a disc. When he was brought into the hospital, he was breathing in short, little, shallow gasps. Of course, he had some lacerations which were easily repaired. It was the rib and lung injuries which were severe. I think it was the first time I had seen the results of punctured lungs. Air escaped from the lungs into the chest cavity. He had such a puffy look on both the back and front of his chest. The first time I attempted to turn him for his comfort, I had this sinking feeling in my stomach. Where ever I touched his upper body the free air would swoosh from one area to another. How thankful that the attending physician was capable and cared for him in a remarkable way. Frankly, I was surprised how quickly he recovered.

One summer, a personable, part-time farmer came into the emergency room with a severely mangled arm. He had become entangled in a grain auger. He was in the hospital a long time. It looked like he would actually lose his entire left arm. It took several operations and surgical procedures followed by painful therapy to restore use of the arm. We became very well acquainted with this likeable man. His wife was about eight months pregnant when the accident occurred. She came in to have their fifth baby while he was recuperating. We put him in a wheel chair and her on the gurney so he could accompany her to the delivery room. He couldn't go in because we were fearful of infection from some of his open wounds. It was one of the happiest moments of his hospitalization. They got a son after four little girls. She was such a quiet, serious little mother. He was talkative and a real tease. Because she seemed to get pregnant so easily, he nicknamed her "old fruitful". I often see this couple on my weekly trips to Stafford and we enjoy greeting one another and having a few good laughs together.

There is a farmer from Stafford who is a real practical joker. He enjoyed pulling stunts on his friends. He had to spend quite a while in the hospital following a rather freakish accident. He was doing fieldwork in the summer. He had just finished coupling up a hydraulic hose when it developed a leak. Without thinking, he automatically grabbed it with his bare hand. Of course, it was under tremendous pressure and shot his hand full of hydraulic oil. We couldn't even see a puncture wound where it entered his hand, but it was about twice the size it should have been. The pain was almost unbearable. His hand continued to get larger and very inflamed. It looked like it would split open. The oil caused a terrible infection. Soon the swelling included his arm. It took days of I.V. medications and treatments to control the infection. When the pain subsided, he looked for ways to tease the nurses. With some outside help, he obtained a piece of plastic contraption which was made to look exactly like the results of vomiting, barfing, upchucking, or puking. When one of the nurses who also likes a practical joke was on duty, he turned on his call light. When she appeared in his room, he acted quite ill and had the "look-like vomitus" laying on his pillow. Her reaction really pleased him and brightened the day for everyone. The nurse kept it for future use. Most of the newly hired nursing employees sooner or later were initiated into our hospital group in the proper way with the help of this gadget.

When I arrived at work at 10:45 one night, the first thing I saw was a pair of cowboy boots, a western type jacket, and a "ten gallon hat". An experienced horseman, a prominent businessman, had been thrown from his horse and received critical head injuries. He had been transferred to Wichita. The clothes were picked up after his death. He had been alone on his horse and no one ever knew what happened.

We had several serious accidents with ranchers attending livestock. I would rather not write about those at this time. There was one fellow who accidentally vaccinated himself for black leg. Cows and calves are not prone to stand still and cooperate for their shots.

A prosperous farmer in the area came into our hospital after a tractor tipped over on him. Of course, his injuries were severe. Because of internal injuries, he could have nothing by mouth. No one, including the doctor, was aware that this man was a habitual drinker of liquor. On his third day following his admittance he went into D.T.s. Oh, it was awful. He ranted and raved, seeing all sorts of things, becoming very difficult to control. At that time there was no specific medication to control such things. If we could have given him a drink it may have helped, but he couldn't tolerate it because of his condition. His general physical condition deteriorated rapidly. Death was the victor.

Since recalling this alcoholic, others come to mind. These patients were ones I dreaded caring for. The first one I had shortly after starting on night duty in the old hospital was one of the worst. The hospital was equipped in an old-fashioned way. Each room had the usual bed or two with a bedside table, but also had an old type dresser with drawers and a large mirror. Shortly after I took over, with no other R.N. near, he began his rampage. It must have been terrible for him. I know it was for me and I didn't see the things he was seeing. He began screaming and was extremely terrified. He saw mice and many other kinds of horrible creatures, hundreds of them. They were overrunning his room. Since they were so thick on the dresser, he was determined to rid his room of them. His strength was phenomenal. He destroyed the dresser, tearing the mirror off and slamming it on his bed. Then he actually tore the woodwork from around the doorframe. I was afraid to stay with him and was afraid to leave. Frantic calls to the attending physician really didn't help much. What an awful night. I am so thankful that there is now medication to help alcoholics through these tough times. Of course, it is also a big help to the nurses.

It seemed that most people addicted to alcohol have pleasant personalities. It was Christmas Eve. I did not want to be working at the hospital. I wanted to be home with my family enjoying this blessed time of year. No other nurse really wanted to be working either. But it was my turn. The doctors informed us earlier that they were sending as many patients home for Christmas as possible. You see, most people preferred not to be hospitalized, at least over the holidays. After the Christmas Eve service in our church, I waited as long as possible to start for Stafford. I arrived exactly on time, not a minute early, and was informed that the patient load was very light and we would have a quiet and easy night. Good news! We had a man in room 112 who had been visiting his family. He was a former resident and now lived in Ohio. Pneumonia struck his body at an inopportune time and three days of treatment had not been enough, so he was spending Christmas with us. He was personable and easy to visit with. Since he was unable to sleep, he often put on his call light. It was necessary for me to be in his room often. I noticed he was becoming rather nervous and jumpy. Maybe it was the season and he missed being with his family. Once again, he called for me. I was standing at his bedside, talking with him, trying to assess his needs and problems. Suddenly, quick as a cat, with no warning, he reached out and slammed me on the bed, face down. I freed myself, backed up and stared at him. He looked extremely excited, his eyes bright and gleaming as he said, "I just saved your life. Didn't you even see the huge beam come crashing through the ceiling right for your head?" I didn't see it or hear it. I just wanted to exit as quickly as possible and slow down my pounding heart. Oh, my, another man with D.T.s. It was NOT a quiet Christmas Eve. The doctor had no idea this man was a chronic drinker. At least at this time, medical progress had produced a drug which could be given to help ease us through the situation.

Intermission

It is fun for me to reminisce about little, unimportant things I encountered while practicing my nursing profession. Names, names, names. I have cared for many "colors". One of my first patients at Stafford was Mr. White. But I have also had a Brown, Black, Redd, Blew, Greene, and Gray. Never did get a Purple. Shucks.

This is the truth. At one time in our hospital, we had women named Flora, Cora, Dora Lora, and Nora. Can you believe they were all there at the same time? Today I have trouble remembering the name of someone I met yesterday. But I can still recall the last names of those five women. Another interesting name situation was the married couple who decided to give their children names starting with letters of the alphabet, beginning with A, etc. and see how far they would get. This is the way it went: Allen, Bruce, Clyde, Della, Elizabeth, Floyd, Grace, Hubert, Ike, Joseph, Karl and Kathy, (twins) and that is when it stopped. What fun!

At one time we noticed some of the last names sounded more like we were in New York than in a little Midwestern town. One night we had Benintendi, Giacoma, Deljanovan, Delgedillo, Gutierrez, and Kurowski. Now doesn't that sound like "foreigners"? Enough of that.

Humor

One of the most important things I learned, and I learned it early, was to laugh. Sometimes we laughed to keep from crying. Many times we tried valiantly to refrain from laughing until we returned to the nurse's station. We were very busy one night years ago. There was an elderly gentleman at the far end of the hall in the last room. He had been quite ill and was rather weak. When his call light was not answered immediately, he decided to go to the bathroom unassisted. He did not make it in time. He urinated and had a large liquid stool all over the floor. Then he proceeded to slip on the wet floor and fall into the mess. He was smeared from heels to shoulders and head. The nurse aide and I hurried to the rescue, but stopped short when we saw the horrible mess. We quickly determined that he was not injured. Next, we tried to decide just what to do. We felt we should get him into bed as quickly as possible, but did not want to get the bed linens soiled. He apologized and was very congenial about the whole matter. We concluded we would bathe him there on the floor, put a clean gown on him and tuck him into a clean bed. The nurse aide filled a large basin with nice warm water and headed for the patient. I stepped into the room with clean linen just in time to see the aide slip on the wet floor. She tried not to fall on the poor man, and because of that valiant effort, she hung onto the basin, but the water shot into the air and landed squarely on the target. The nurse aide was on the floor right by the thoroughly soused patient. He began to laugh and exclaimed about the new method of giving showers. We all three enjoyed a wonderful laugh together. What a remarkable man. He could have gotten irate, but instead he helped us all have a good time during a bad experience. We finally accomplished our goal: getting him clean, dry, and comfortable.

In the same area of the hospital at about the same time we were caring for a woman who had been quite ill. She was finally recovering, but would occasionally become confused and would wander from her room. Prior to this night we were concerned about her problem with chronic constipation. On this night, she wandered down the hall while we were having our fun time in 112. She apparently heard our laughter and headed our way. She was scantily clad as so many hospital people are. She dropped the Kleenex she was carrying right in front of the room we were in. When she stooped over to pick up her "hankie" she shot these little bullets across the hall, hitting the opposite wall. Again, we had reason to laugh and laugh and clean and clean. What fun we had that night.

Nurses occasionally find humor in unusual situations. Laughter at inappropriate times can be difficult for other people to understand. It was not unusual for the nurses in our small hospital to be well acquainted with our patients. Many times after the death of a patient, nurses would attend the funeral or at least visit the mortuary. One of our elderly, frequent patients had expired. My dear nurse friend, June, and I decided we would miss sleep and pay a visit to the mortuary in a neighboring town. This person had been a bit demanding with the nurses and had occasionally scolded June, who happened to be a distant relative. On the way to the funeral home, we had a pleasant visit recalling our dealings with this man. We were met as we entered the mortuary by a finely attired, rather sober, stern-looking funeral director. The open casket was placed in the front of the chapel. No one else was present, except the serious director. We walked the long, heavily carpeted aisle to the casket. June looked at the body of this man and gently reached down to touch his hand. Ohhhh, static electricity had built up on our walk down the aisle. When she touched the hand of our "patient", there was a rather loud pop and sparks flew at us. We both jumped back as June exclaimed, "Oh, he got me again." Then we began to laugh and laugh and laugh. In the back of the chapel was the unsmiling man, arms folded across his chest, glaring at two women who were laughing hysterically while they viewed a corpse.

I was not the only night nurse who was troubled with sleep interruptions. No one really delighted in working the graveyard shift. Maxine is one of my dear friends. She is pretty, petite, and very feminine. She had a terrible time trying to adjust to the night shift. She would get quite tired. When we got that way, we quickly realized how very important our rest was. We needed rest and sleep to be alert on the job. One summer, she was placed on the dreaded third shift for a few nights. She was tired. She was sleepy. She got home one morning, exhausted, and quickly crawled into bed. Her husband and son loved peacocks and had some on the farm. Have you ever heard peacocks call, screech, and make noise in general? They can almost have a human sound. She had just gotten to sleep, when a peacock parked in a tree outside her window began calling, loudly. That did it! She was tired. Now she was angry. Out of bed, in a huff. Her husband and son were a bit shocked to see this small woman in her shorty nightgown grab her husband's shotgun, go charging outside and blast that peacock out of the tree. The peacock didn't die, so Maxine grabbed a nearby hoe and began chopping the poor bird's head off. She was still angry and used the hoe so violently that it broke. The peacock died. All was quiet. Maxine went to bed.

One night years ago, I had a most unusual experience. The hospital was almost full. We were busy. I was the only R.N. on duty. One of our patients was an alcoholic woman about my age. I think she had succeeded in destroying a few too many brain cells with her excessive drinking. I was glad she was quiet and cooperative that night because I was so busy. Shortly after five o'clock in the morning, the telephone rang. I dreaded the thought of a new patient. I was surprised to hear a man ask if all our patients were in the hospital and accounted for. His dog had awakened him and was a bit excited. When he went into his living room, he discovered a female in a short, red nightgown asleep on his couch. We quickly checked. Sure enough, this woman's bed was empty. I sent one of my two helpers down the street to bring this wanderer back into the fold. I admit that I felt embarrassed.

Reactions to Death

Shortly after I began working the night shift with no other R.N. in the hospital, I felt a little uneasy to be on my own. The responsibility seemed a bit heavy as I realized I was actually accountable for the well being of humans in life and death situations. I was caring for an elderly woman, Ruth, who was dying from cancer. Her devoted son had arrived from Georgia to be with her. She knew her time was growing short. He knew death was near. We had talked about it. I felt like everyone was ready and prepared. I was even feeling almost comfortable that my first experience of this kind, where I was totally responsible, was so expected. This son sat by his Mother's bed for three nights in a row. I offered coffee frequently and we had some good visits and became acquainted. I'm sorry to say I was not prepared when death crept in that fourth night. Ruth died. I told the son it was over. Since he had been waiting all those days, knowing that the death of his mother was inevitable, I thought that would be it. Simple. Not so. He broke down completely. His body shook with horrible, uncontrollable sobs. I certainly did not expect this and hadn't prepared myself well at all. I struggled through the necessary things in an inept fashion. I felt ashamed and vowed that from now on I would always be prepared and ready for ANY situation. Any type reaction to death was not going to surprise me.

Always be prepared was my motto. There was a married couple who had spent almost fifty years together. The husband had a heart attack and was recovering nicely. His faithful wife came to see him every day, without fail. She drove her own car, but often brought a friend with her. Her attire was impeccable with expensive clothes and an ever-present hat. In fact, she had quite an assortment of hats. Spending many hours at his bedside, she seemed very devoted. What a lovely picture. One morning, shortly after giving early morning care just before shift change, I went into his room again and was shocked to see he had expired. It was so unexpected, I spent some time working over him and making sure he was dead. I took a deep breath, gathered my thoughts, and made the dreaded phone call. The physician warned me not to tell the older wife that her husband was dead. We were to ask her to come right away because his condition had changed dramatically. I was supposed to be off duty before she had time to arrive, but it was necessary and required that I stay to finish the case. Remembering Ruth and her son, I steeled myself for the ordeal. What a blow for this woman who had spent all those years with this man. I was as ready as I could be when she arrived, dressed in all her finery, even a hat. As gently as I could, I greeted her, put my arm around her shoulders, and quietly informed her that her husband had passed away. She stopped short, and exclaimed, "Oh, so he finally died." Then she turned to her friend and said, "Well, we might as well go home." I thought I was ready, but not for that. I asked her if she wouldn't like to go to his room and see him one more time. She shrugged her shoulders and simply said she saw no need of that. After that experience, I made another vow. I would be ready for anything and not be surprised. SURPRISE!

Yes, I was not going to be shocked at any reaction again. In another case, I do not remember the name like I do the other ones, but do I ever recall the incident! Our patient was an older woman, but not real elderly. She was in the slow process of dying. The doctor had called all her children home because death was inevitable. Since nurses spend much more time with hospitalized patients than physicians do, they could sometimes anticipate the actual time of death. Of course, no one can predict accurately to the hour. The entire troupe of relatives came to the nurse's station to talk with me. They asked if she was going to die that night. Of course I could not give a positive time. I supposed they wanted to take turns, so everyone would not have to become worn out. No, their request was entirely different. They all wanted to go home to sleep, but they did want to be present at the time of her passing. They were quite emphatic and wanted me to call them so they would have time to return to the hospital for the "event". They proceeded to explain the reason. None of them had ever seen anyone die, and they all wanted to be there to witness this exciting event. No one mentioned wanting to be with their mother as a source of comfort or just to show their love. I felt like an icy blast just hit my heart. They must have had ice water running through their veins. I told them to go on home, but I could not promise they would be called in time. I immediately decided if it looked like her time was near, I would move very slowly to the telephone. Somehow, I did not relish giving those uncaring children the pleasure and excitement of "seeing someone die". Once again, I was surprised by fellow human beings, just in a different way.

D. and T. had been married a number of years. Were they happy? How can we know? It seemed they got most of their enjoyment in life by bickering and fussing. He was a small, wispy man with a hooked nose. She was a rather pretty lady with a nice complexion. Separately, they were both pleasant and congenial. When they spent time together, the fur flew. D. developed a serious heart condition which necessitated hospitalization. Naturally, D. died on my shift. At three o'clock in the morning, the Doctor escorted T. into the hospital with the sad news. Doctor had his arm around her as they walked down the hall to D.'s room. What a commotion as they slowly made their way down that long hall. One step, a not so quiet scream, "D.," next step, a loud cry, "NO." Every step meant a loud emotional agonizing yell, "D., no, D., no", etc. I followed along trying to put the soft pedal on. It was no fun for this nurse to have 25 wide-awake patients asking questions and spending the rest of the night with numerous requests. Maybe D. and T. really did love each other and just had a strange way of showing it.

Between two and three o'clock one morning a lovely lady from Sylvia brought her husband into the hospital. When I asked what the problem was, he replied simply that he was dying. Then he began to sing in a loud vigorous voice, "Now when the saints go marching in, when the saints go marching in, I want to be in that number, when the saints go marching in." His wife tried to hush him to no avail. He was happy. He was elated. He was excited because he was going home. The doctor was called. A brief exam did reveal a problem. Treatment was instigated. He continued to lustily sing his song, while holding his hand in the air. I thought to myself, "You old coot, if you can sing like that, you aren't about to die. Be quiet and go to sleep." At seven o'clock, I was glad to head for home. When I returned to work that night, I didn't see his name on the patient records. When I asked about him, the nurse said, "Oh, he died this morning." I could hardly believe it. As a postscript to this little story, I was surprised to see this widow lady at our church when we celebrated our centennial. She told me how impressed she was with the sermon which was delivered by my son, Kent.

Mrs. L. was in her eighties and had a wonderful personality with a delightful sense of humor. Even though she suffered from a serious heart disease, I enjoyed caring for her. One night she told me she was weary with her life's struggle. She was ready to quit the gallant effort and go be with her Lord. I could understand her feelings. Later that night I was startled while making rounds when I got to her room. I found her up on her knees in the middle of the bed, with her arms stretched into the air. Her eyes were closed and she was praying audibly. Even though I was afraid she might pitch right off the bed, I hesitated to interrupt that prayer. Over and over, she was requesting God to take her, repeating that she was ready. "Take me, Lord, take me." Finally, she flopped back on the bed and rather disgustedly said, "Well (blankity-blank), God, take me." I smiled and thought how many times we desire our prayers to be answered immediately. It took several days before she had her prayer answered.

A difficult, busy night ended with an unforgettable death. A nice couple, a little older than my husband and I, were parents of two boys. One of them was tragically, profoundly retarded. The other boy was a sweet young fellow, in spite of epilepsy, which was being controlled with medication. Time passed and the parents were enjoying this son. He became ill when he was in his late teens. He was diagnosed with cancer of the stomach. In spite of surgery and the available treatment, this dreaded disease marched on in its destructive way. His condition worsened and he was hospitalized for bleeding from the upper intestinal tract. That last night blood transfusions were administered. A tube was placed through his nose into the stomach to relieve vomiting. It seemed to me we were losing blood faster than we could replace it. The battle was being lost. I was the only nurse on duty with many patients in my care. It was time for numerous 6:00 medications to be administered. Of course, the parents had spent the night with their son. I felt it was quite necessary for me to exit the room to call for another nurse to come early to help with medications. The mother begged me not to leave. It did appear their son was dying. I called my trusted nurse aide in and requested her to make phone calls for me. The young man was conscious and talking with his mother. Once again she asked me to stay at the bedside with them. It was very difficult and emotional for everyone in the room. The dying boy said his vision was failing, everything was getting dark. Then he said it was getting harder to hear us talk. His mother kept talking to him in a reassuring way, telling him Jesus would care for him. While all this was transpiring at the bedside, the poor distraught father stood at the doorway of the room, repeatedly bumping his head against the doorframe. Even though I felt a terrible need to go to the agitated father, I stayed by my patient, doing what I could for his comfort. I believe the last words the young man heard were that Jesus would not leave him. He would always be there to care for him. It was all over before the extra nurse arrived. This family made a positive impression on me.

One other tough situation of this type concerned a young mother of 10 children. The oldest was about 16 years old, the youngest just babies (twins). The mother had been in a car accident and was slowly recovering from her injuries. She was almost ready to be dismissed to go home. Early in the morning, the dreaded thing happened. The nurse aide went into her room and discovered the woman had expired. It most likely was a blood clot from the injury which dislodged and moved to the heart. Once again, I had that dreaded awful job of notifying the family. The husband came immediately. He was much older and a hardened, crusty, foul talking man. He brought his two older sons with him. I met them in the chapel and sympathetically gave them the sad news. The father was surprisingly nice to me. After visiting about the necessary things, he very gruffly ordered his sons to "Go see your mother." They were very quiet. They were sober. They did not move. Again, the father demanded they go see their mom. Still they did not move. I asked them if they would like me to go with them. They eagerly nodded their heads. We walked hand in hand into the room. The visit was brief, quiet, with no tears. It was so difficult for them. They wanted to act like their dad – a "real" man. I wanted them to weep a little. They were only boys.

Memorable Patients

Many years ago, a wandering hobo type person appeared at the hospital door. His clothes were dirty, but not too full of holes. His shoes were coming apart and extremely stiff and harsh from walking in water too often. These shoes (or lack of them) had rubbed sores on his feet. These lesions were open, draining, and badly infected. He had difficulty walking. The kind doctor admitted him to the hospital for antibiotic treatment of his infected feet. Then he ordered all his clothes to be laundered by the hospital laundry workers. Next, he gave one of the male employees some money and sent him to the local clothing store to buy a supply of white socks for the man. It had been a long time since that man had had socks to protect his feet. When his feet had improved with daily baths, treatment, and T.L.C., he was dismissed to go merrily on his way down the highway. What kind of pay did the Doctor receive? A deep sense of satisfaction in knowing he had helped one of the least of these, my brethren. We certainly appreciated those old fashioned physicians.

T. was an older, rather cantankerous, moderately wealthy lady. She was tall and strong looking in spite of health problems. There was a bit of a mean streak running through this female. One cold winter night, she asked for a glass of ice water. My co-worker gladly responded to the request, because T. seemed to be getting weaker. Norma leaned over T. to offer a drink. Of course, T. wanted to hold the glass herself. Quick as a cat, showing no sign of weakness, T. threw the entire glass of ice water in Norma's face. What a shock! Norma's brown eyes flashed and glared. I really think she came very close to popping her patient a good one. Nurses are not supposed to abuse their patients, but should patients be allowed to abuse their caregivers? T.'s heart was not responding to treatment so she had to stay with us. UGH! Because of a condition which caused her feet to drop, making walking difficult or impossible, we were to keep tennis shoes on her day and night. The shoes provided were too large for even her big feet. She never wanted to be covered with a sheet or blanket. It always looked so funny to walk into her room or down the hall and see those huge tennis shoes sticking up on the feet of that gray haired lady. Those shoes must have given her a feeling of power, a weapon, perhaps. One night, we had to move her to another room because her poor roommate had reached the saturation point of endurance. This placed her next to a window. Later, when she became angry with this nurse, a common daily occurrence, she gave a mighty kick with that large, shoe clad foot. This nurse adeptly stepped aside, which allowed the foot to go crashing through the window. What a racket! A shower of glass fell on our dear T. I could imagine all kinds of deep lacerations and injuries. Not a scratch. We never put her near a window again. Our nights were a little more pleasant after her departure. What a woman!

V. was a pretty middle aged lady who had numerous physical complaints. She seemed to desire to be a patient in the hospital. Insecure and dependent, her abdominal pain was increasing. A nurse from her hometown informed us that her husband apparently had another love in his life. We wondered if there was a connection. One night, I was making my routine rounds, checking on the welfare of my patients. V.'s bed was empty. The room was dark, but I could tell the bathroom door was open. No one was in the bathroom. Then I heard her. Behind the bathroom door, tucked in the corner sat V. Very quietly and softly, she was singing, "Brighten the corner where you are" while gently clapping her hands to keep time with her song. Either she did not see me or was simply ignoring me. At any rate, she just kept singing her little song in her dark corner. What an unusual way for this adult woman to try to brighten her corner.

A slow talking, slow moving elderly man lived alone in a remote rural area of Stafford County. He decided to clean up the place where he was residing. He needed to burn a small pile of trash and brush. He had a good fire started and did not notice it was creeping through dry grass toward him. Not only was he slow moving and slow talking but also slow thinking. The fire didn't blaze up, but got his high top shoes warm enough to begin to slowly burn. Perhaps the blood vessels and nerves in his lower extremities were affected by cirrhosis or something. He hardly seemed aware that his shoes were burning. We were shocked to see that his shoes had actually burned off his feet. Of course the burns extended deep into his feet. It was strange that he could keep his other clothes from burning. We were certainly dealing with an unusual man. He showed no emotion when both feet had to be amputated. He appeared to have absolutely no feelings, either physical or emotional. With no family to help him, he spent his remaining days in a rest home.

A routine hospital day began in March. The controlled routine suddenly became frantic activity with the admission of the young wife of a local minister. She had just suffered a massive heart attack and quickly went into cardiac arrest. The physician was present and instigated the immediate necessary treatment. Of course, CPR was started. The proper heart medication was given intravenously. CPR had to be continued. With each injection of medication, everyone was watching and hoping for response from the heart. Perhaps there was a little action for a minute, then nothing. CPR had to be continued. When two people would become exhausted from giving CPR, two fresh hospital employees would take over. Many hospital workers thought the battle was lost, but the doctor would not give up. Keep working! For two hours, the exhausting, stressful, tense activity continued. The determination of the physician and the extremely hard work of hospital employees finally proved effective. The woman's heart began to function on its own. She had to be in intensive care for many days, as her condition was precarious. Even though her speech and actions were a bit impaired for a time, she eventually recovered fully. The doctor and nurses were at first completely exhausted, then exhilarated. How truly exciting and awesome to be a part in helping extend the life of a person in her prime. This patient eventually recovered fully and moved with her husband to another state. The following year, another routine hospital day in March arrived. The owner of the local flower shop made a delivery to the nurse's station. The vase contained two carnations and a package of LifeSavers candy. The gift card had no name, only the following message, "Thank you for another year of life." Nurses were puzzled and very curious. Who sent this? The employees in medical records searched the files. Yes, on this date, the minister's wife had entered the hospital and remembered the heroic efforts which had saved her life. That occurred years ago, but every year, on that date, two carnations and a package of LifeSavers candy arrive at the hospital. It is so nice to be remembered and appreciated.

Suicide Attempts

Doctors and nurses spend years and much effort getting an education for the purpose of saving lives or making final days more meaningful and bearable. It is interesting but sad to see so many people of all ages who take or attempt to take their own lives. I was a bit surprised how often this happened in a small, rural setting. These were difficult situations for medical personnel as well as relatives of the person who wanted to exit this life.

Nighttime and darkness must be especially difficult for sad and depressed people. It seemed so many suicide attempts occurred at night when the night shift was on duty at the hospital. And I worked this night shift. Just before midnight in the winter many years ago, three kids came to the emergency door. The eighth grade boy had driven the car and was accompanied by a fifth grade sister and a little girl who was about six-years-old. The boy was stoic, the girls were weeping. They had managed to get their unresponsive, semi-conscious mother into the car because she wouldn't (couldn't) talk to them. They were scared. Dad was out on the town. He had to have his usual round of drinks. The police did a quick check and found evidence that she had consumed a large dose of a potent drug. We spent time doing gastric lavage, discovering the medications had already been absorbed into her system. She was becoming increasingly comatose. After admitting this mother into the hospital and beginning I.V. fluids, the

113

physician took the three children into an empty room for a visit. He cradled the youngest in his arms on his lap and attempted to comfort and reassure them. He kept telling them that their mother was going to be okay while I was thinking that statement was a bit premature. The woman appeared critical. The doctor did not want these youngsters to return home to await a drunken father, but they had no other relatives in the area. He told us to put them to bed in an empty room and he would pay for the use of the room. The boy refused to stay. He spoke almost no words the entire time he was with us. The older girl quietly wept. The youngest kept crying, "Don't let my mommy die." She didn't die, but she was unconscious for three whole days. Poor traumatized kids!

I soon learned that women almost always used drugs or medication if they wanted to end their life. Men were determined to do it in a violent, but more effective way. Some were careful and "thoughtful" in selecting the time and place. One man decided to shoot himself in the abdomen in his own bedroom. I guess he wanted his wife to have to clean up the mess. Of course, he didn't die right away. We spent frantic energy and much time in surgery. He died after incurring a large medical bill.

One man in the area decided to end it all. He would also use a gun. He wouldn't go for the abdomen. A more sure way would be to shoot himself in the head. So he did! He was brought into the hospital with part of his skull missing and his brain damaged, but he was very much alive. He recovered, but was partially paralyzed and continued to behave in a weird fashion. He could walk. As a matter of fact, he could run, with a limp. Some people were fearful of him, but I considered him harmless. I almost changed my mind one night. He was a patient occupying a room at the far end of the hall. Hearing a commotion, I stepped into the hall and saw this strange sight. This man was running up the hall, his hospital gown unbuttoned and on backwards, flapping in the breeze. He sped right by me, running pell mell into the chapel, lowered his head, and crashed into the wall. He was using his head like a billy goat. He bounced back halfway across the room landing on his back. I thought it might have killed him, especially since it broke a glass brick in the wall which was about eight inches thick. I helped him up and he quietly walked back to his room. I do believe he had the hardest head in this country.

Suicide! A woman in her early forties chose an interesting method when she became tired of the "rat race". She swallowed a large amount of rat poison. I guess she didn't realize just what it did to rats. When she began to bleed from many body orifices, it was frightening. She didn't know she might bleed from her ears and eyes. Going for help seemed the thing to do. Treatment with intravenous medications to counteract the bleeding worked. She even decided she might like to live a while longer.

Several high school students attempted suicide, some in a rather feeble way. Most all of them used overdoses of medications. Not long before I retired, a teenager was brought in after swallowing 30 Tylenol. He waited for hours before deciding to tell someone so he wouldn't die. After flushing his system with copious amounts of I.V. fluids, the doctor told him that he didn't kill himself, but he had just killed his liver. The outlook was not good.

An intelligent, interesting man was a patient in our hospital in the coronary care unit. The prognosis for this man was not good. He was a veteran of W.W. II where he had become an outstanding pilot. He was very egotistical, and an assertive, take-charge guy. He attempted to control everything and everyone. Since he did not sleep well at night, I found myself in his room often and for long periods. I must admit I rather enjoyed hearing stories of flying experiences during the war. He was given the task of teaching pilots for combat. He mentioned several famous names of individuals he had trained. At one time he asked me if I would like to know the very best and most capable man he ever saw in a plane. Of course, I wanted to know. He smiled. It was almost a smirk as he said, "Me." This man was quite difficult to care for because he was so demanding and hatefully bossy. He was certainly showing his authority. He was in charge! I think his prognosis was heavy on his mind. The doctor finally gave permission for this vet to go home. His last night in the hospital was so different. He was kind, sweet, thoughtful and very appreciative. I couldn't believe how really nice he was. The next day his wife took him home. Later that morning, she went to take a shower. While she had the water running, he took a gun, shot, and killed himself. Always in charge.

Some people who are intent on committing suicide are forced into shrewd intricate plans. I am thankful that this next event did not happen when and where I was in charge. A middle-aged man was a patient in the hospital and showed no serious signs of depression. His wife was visiting him one afternoon. He informed her a friend of the family had been in to see him and was interested in buying one of his guns. He wanted to see it first. Since this friend was coming back soon, the wife was requested to bring the weapon to the hospital so it could be sold. She granted his request. No nurse saw or was aware of this activity. It would certainly have been frowned on. That night he placed the gun in his mouth, fired it, and got the nurse's attention.

Insignificant Memories

Occasionally, violent storms roared in the night skies to frighten patients and workers alike. One night we had a full patient load. Two boys were combatting pneumonia and were sharing a room. One was a teenager, the other one about four years old. I was making rounds at the height of the storm and found the bed of the little fellow vacant. He was frightened and had crawled into bed with the BIG boy. The older lad had his arm around the young kid in a very protective manner. He did not even complain when the four-year-old got so scared that he wet the bed.

A similar thing occurred on another stormy night. This time it was two little old ladies who were in their eighties. They were obviously frightened and were in the same bed, cuddled up tightly together. They were very unwilling to return to separate beds. I guess they felt they could really protect each other.

It didn't always take a storm for patients to share a bed. One night a confused older male patient was lonely and wandered into a female's room. This lady was a very frail, fragile person known for her whining ways. The man crawled into her bed and was actually on top of her. Of course they were both fully dressed and had a sheet and blanket between them. Nevertheless, it brought weak, pitiful little cries for help. We got him back to his room quickly. She did not even appear very upset. Maybe she enjoyed a bit of excitement in her dull routine.

117

Other situations along these lines were not so innocent and harmless. One local citizen was prohibited from ever visiting the hospital because he was seen molesting a slightly retarded young girl. We were surprised because this man was a frequent and faithful visitor of so many sick and ailing people of the community.

One interesting little episode which made nurses laugh happened on my shift. A patient had expired (this was not the humorous part) and our duty was to notify a mortuary from a neighboring town. The funeral director arrived at the emergency drive with a helper. They were quite congenial and happy. As a matter of fact, they were a little inebriated. They had to walk the length of two long halls. In order to help their staggering gait, they each had to lean on the wall or reach their hand on the wall every step. We had to help them load the body for removal. We watched with uneasiness as they drove off. Sure enough, we later heard they ended up in the ditch. We were glad the dead body received no injuries.

Working in a hospital in a small town meant caring for relatives, friends, acquaintances, and occasionally total strangers. Sometimes strange strangers. One middle-aged fellow traveled down highways on foot apparently living off the land and perhaps the kindness of people. He began having severe health problems. He was troubled with shortness of breath, wheezing, and edematous extremities. As he got into Stafford, he found a Doctor's office and a caring physician. His feet and legs were so swollen he had trouble walking. He was placed in the hospital and treated for congestive heart failure. With medications, rest, and T.L.C., his condition improved, but he certainly wasn't well enough to be dismissed. We began to wonder where he would go, how he could survive life on the road, and how he could pay his bill. At least one of these questions was easily answered. It was my night to work; I always tried to make rounds of all patient rooms at least every hour. Wakeful patients became accustomed to the routine and could anticipate my approach. This particular night, as I neared his room, I sensed activity. But as I entered the room, I found him in bed with the sheet tucked under his chin. His face was turned to the wall and his eyes were closed. Something did not appear right. I felt so sure that he was awake, trying to look asleep. I watched him for a while. Why did I have such a strong feeling that I had interrupted frantic activity? If he was indeed asleep, I didn't want to awaken him. Because of an uneasy feeling, I decided to check on him in a short time. This time I found the bed empty, his closet empty, and the window open. He found a way to avoid paying the hospital bill. Soon after that, the entire window system was changed. Double panes were installed and fixed so it was impossible to open enough to permit a person to make a grand exit.

Some things are difficult to explain. In this very same room, several years later, an eerie thing occurred. The mother-in-law of one of the nurse's aides was recovering from a bout of pneumonia. She was preparing for dismissal. I was returning to the nurse's station after giving another patient an injection. I noticed this patient was returning to bed from the bathroom. Wanting to make sure everything was okay, I stopped in to check on her. We visited for a while. No problems, all was fine. As I was leaving, she asked if I would return to check on her again. I assured her I would. Then she asked me to promise I would come in 30 minutes. It seemed a strange request, but I agreed. When I returned, she was positioned exactly as she was when I left, only this time she was dead! What a shock – to me, to the doctor, and to the nurse's aide. The physician drove the ten miles to the home of this woman with the daughter-in-law on that cold, snowy, winter night to be with the family. I

119

was left to wonder if she sensed impending death or even if this was some unusual method of suicide.

One of my favorite patients was an elderly gentleman who was a Native American and had the typical physical appearance of one. This impressed me. He and his wife had been married for 70 years and remained extremely devoted to one another. They acted like two lovebirds. Illness struck the wife at Thanksgiving time. The hospital employees all worked together to make this a special time for them. A small table was placed in the room by the bed. A white linen tablecloth and special dishes and silverware were provided. Someone even found a nice candle to add to the atmosphere. They enjoyed their last very special Thanksgiving dinner together, with their heads nearly touching as they ate the meal together. This man's wife died soon after that special meal together. This gentle man mourned for the lost love of his life. He continued to live alone with frequent visits from his granddaughter. Some time later the granddaughter brought him into the hospital because he was having a problem with his heart. She was leaving just as I was getting to work one night. We stopped for a visit at the front door. We discussed his condition. She was aware of the warm relationship her Granddad and I had. As she left, she said, "Well, I won't worry about him tonight because you are here." I wished she had not said that. At two o'clock in the morning, I was going to the room at the end of the hall to administer an I.V. medication which took about ten minutes. As I passed his room, I noticed he was awake so I stopped briefly, gave an exaggerated wave and told him I would stop in and talk on my way back. He gave me a big smile, waved and nodded his head. On my return trip up the hall, a quick glance into the room made my heart sink and pulse race. I was immediately aware that something was wrong. I hurried into the room. A quick check with my stethoscope indicated that there was no sign of life in my old pal. I did not want to make that phone call to the relative who felt no need to worry because I was on duty. We were both comforted by the easy way he made his exit from this life.

Many years ago, when I began working several nights a week, I was still young, almost wrinkle-free, had no gray hair, and had very little extra weight – in other words I looked much different than I do now. Two young men of the area were driving their pick-ups and had a violent meeting at an intersection. They were brought into the hospital with serious injuries. At that time we were still caring for almost all types of patients and were not sending them to bigger facilities. These two men were a challenge to care for because of their severe injuries. I remember they both had broken shoulder blades, which I thought was unusual. One of these patients could do very little for himself and had to have almost complete care. After two or three weeks, he had improved enough to use one arm. One night I was leaning over him, changing a dressing on his neck and shoulder. I was really concentrating on my work, so was not prepared for a romantic interlude. Rather quickly, his good arm flew around my neck, and he pulled me down and planted a long lingering kiss on my cheek. I was a wee bit angry and left the room in a big hurry. My nurse aides immediately knew something was wrong. I told them they were to care for this man from now on. I would go in for things that only a registered nurse could do. Very soon his call light came on. I told one of my aides to answer. She soon returned to report the patient wanted to see me. I told Vera to take care of his requests. Again she returned saying he really needed to talk to me. I went in. He apologized profusely. I accepted his apology and was able to care for him until he recovered and was dismissed. I never mentioned this to my hubby. Occasionally, I see this man and wonder if he remembers our close encounter. I do. He doesn't act like he even knows me. I am glad.

Why did it seem like most often our patients died at night? I hope it wasn't poorer nursing care. Perhaps it was just more appropriate for people to slip out of this world during the darkness of night. A prominent businessman from a neighboring town was dying from cancer. His wife and son were spending much time with him. The wife had gone home to try to get some much-needed rest. The son was about 12 years younger than me. He was attentive, pleasant, and caring. I was spending as much time in the room as I could without neglecting other patients. The man died in the early morning hour. The son accepted it very nicely. We took care of all the necessary business, made the needed phone calls, and the young man waited for the mortician to arrive. This gave me time to catch up on my charting and do the necessary work to complete his chart. I was absorbed and certainly did not hear the young man enter the nurses' station behind my back. I was startled when he threw his arms around me - tightly - and proceeded to give me kisses on the cheek. He hurriedly explained that it was for being so nice to him during a trying time. I felt it was a bit unusual to show his appreciation in this way.

Drug Users

It was the middle of the night. Things were quiet so we decided to have our "meal" and coffee. The quiet was very short-lived. Suddenly we heard this terrible crash and breaking glass. We rushed to the lobby to find the entire glass in the front door shattered with shreds of glass over the entire lobby floor. A wild-eyed, bare-footed young man was trembling and cowering against the wall. His feet were bleeding from running across the broken glass. He seemed unaware of that fact. He was extremely frightened because of the horrible things he was seeing. He begged for help from the nurses. All he had really wanted was to find a little excitement so he merely tried an illegal hallucinogen. My, did it work. He became so frantic; he decided to rush to the hospital. At least he knew where it was. There was one little problem with his mental function. His vision indicated he was about ¼ mile from the hospital door. In reality he was about 25 yards. He was desperate. Speed was imperative. He hit the hospital door full force, thinking he was still far away. We were thankful his only injuries were lacerations on his feet. The physician quickly tended to the repair work. The big problem was what to do with the patient until the drug wore off. We had to keep him around for a while. There were many very surprised hospital employees when they arrived at work that day. Some even changed their minds about the dull life on the night shift.

That same front door was the scene of another wild episode for me. Due to the changing times, we were instructed to keep the outside doors locked at all times after 11:00 p.m. Shortly after midnight, five young men suddenly began banging on the door and yelling LOUDLY. They were extremely intoxicated and excited. I immediately noticed that one of them had a very obviously broken arm. He was in much pain. His drunken buddies kept jerking on the door. It was impossible for me to unlock it as long as it was being jerked. They yelled at me. I yelled at them to let go of the door so I could let them in. Instead, they screamed and swore at me. One of them said if I couldn't open the door, he would. He proceeded to jerk the door so violently that the entire locking device pulled out of the door. They got in. Their demeanor and behavior improved as they received help. The maintenance supervisor couldn't believe what he saw when he got to work at seven that morning. He thought it would be physically impossible for someone to do that much damage. It took awhile for that to be repaired. He then added another device which he assured us would be more foolproof.

Our sons were in high school. I never felt undue concern about them being tempted to use drugs. When several high schoolers were admitted to our facility with overdoses, I still felt like our kids would know better. Why do people want to chance destroying their brains with potent drugs? One of the high school kids very nearly succeeded in wiping out his brain. He was brought in completely wild and berserk. We spent several terrible days and nights trying to control this young lad. We thought it was bad, but it must have been absolutely horrible for him. One night he cowered under his bed, thinking there was a terrible fire all around him. We couldn't coax him out. Later, we were very busy with other patients. When we checked on him, he was gone. We began a frantic search. Do you have any idea how many places there are in the hospital for someone to hide? We began to methodically go from room to room in every area of the entire building. We were certain he would not leave the place of his protection. Finally, with much relief, we found him in a closet next to the delivery room in the O.B. department. He tried to hold the door shut, because he was fearful of the wild beasts that were after him. What a relief when his body was finally cleared of the drug. I wondered if he would be able to function in a normal manner and live a useful life. I still get occasional reports of this person and he is doing better than we expected.

We were experiencing a very busy night at the hospital. Nearly every bed was full. I was the only R.N. on duty, but I had two of the best nurse aides. We certainly wanted no accident or E.R. patients that night. It seemed we were constantly running from room to room caring for our needy people. The young man who appeared at the front door, clad only in a pair of shorts, was not what we really wanted to see. He was filled with panic, begging us to help him get the drugs out of his system. It was not that simple. The doctor was actually willing to come see him at that very inconvenient hour. After a visit with the "experimenter", and an exam, the doctor told him to go home and let it wear off. The doctor left. The boy didn't. He was *so* scared and absolutely refused to leave. I called the physician again asking what we should do. He said it was either home or jail, and felt it should not be jail. Just send him home! But if he would not go, just let him sit in the lobby. I explained the situation to our nearly naked young man, took him to the lobby and tried to make him comfy. He was cold, which was understandable. We provided a warm blanket and offered a pillow. I hurried back to my other work. As I was rushing down the hall with medication for a "real" patient, I had a strange sensation and looked back. There on my heels was this bare-footed, blanket-draped, wild-eyed boy. He was too frightened to stay alone. I firmly informed him he could not go with me as I cared for my patients. He waited in the hall. When I finally sat down in the nurse's station to chart, I found him directly behind me sitting cross-legged on the floor with his blanket. It reminded me of an Indian. He wanted to stay so close to me – so he could reach out and touch me. Everywhere I went, he was on my heels. At least he agreed not to enter a patient room. What a night! He was my constant shadow the whole night. When it began to get daylight, he was somewhat less fearful and finally agreed to go home. I hope he learned a lesson.

One drug user caused me to lose sleep even though I never met or saw him. A phone call came in the middle of the night. The male caller sounded mature and educated. He told me he had tried a drug for the first time. He was frightened because of the strange and terrible feelings he was experiencing. He wanted help. I suggested he come to the hospital and I would call his physician. He was afraid to do that because he was sure I would call the police. He refused to give his name or location. I tried to convince him I would not notify the police. We talked at length. He continued to plead for help. "Can't you tell me what to do to get this out of my system?" He seemed to get some sense of reassurance merely by talking on the phone. His vivid descriptions of his feelings certainly impressed me. He continued to refuse to come for help. He was so fearful authorities would discover his identity. I was concerned about what might happen to this man. We were required to write any unusual happening in our night report. Of course, I wrote this in a brief way, went home, and tried to forget it. Getting restful, adequate sleep in the daytime was always a problem. Following this episode, I had been asleep about two hours when my phone rang. It was the director of nurses. She had read my report, become quite concerned, and called all the administrative personnel together for a discussion. They hashed this over for thirty minutes trying to decide what I should have done while I was on the phone with this troubled man. They made this momentous decision. It was suggested that I should have sent my nurse's aide to another phone to call the operator and have this phone call traced. They had so many questions. How old did I think he was? Did he use proper language? On and on with questions and suggestions. I will admit we were all a bit fearful we might hear about a death from drug overdose. I was upset for two reasons. My sleep was interrupted. What bothered me more than that was having them tell me what I should have done on the spur of the moment while I was trying to talk sense with an agitated man. Several of them sat quietly in an office putting their ideas together with no distraction of a phone conversation. Oh well, no one died. There was just one tired, sleepy nurse that night.

The hospital was almost full. Some patients were restless and wakeful. Suddenly we heard this terrible banging noise coming from the emergency driveway. Patient call lights came on. Several wanted to inform us that someone was trying to come into the hospital. Of course, we soon discovered the problem when a police officer came in, excitedly telling us they needed help with this wild, violent young man they had in the police car. Too many drugs had caused him to begin violent, destructive behavior on the streets. It took several officers to finally get him in the car. He had been injured days earlier and had his leg in a cast which he was using as a weapon. He was beating on the door and interior of the car. He was screaming obscenities. All the policemen and extra officers that had been called in were also screaming and yelling at the young man. It was quite a wild scene. Not one person was talking in a normal voice. The doctor on call told me to give this man a very potent sedative, which was normally used for drug users. He casually told me to just give the injection while the patient was in the car. Oh, yes, easy! He added that he would come down to the hospital after awhile. How nice. As I fixed the injection, I listened to all the screaming and cursing. It seemed obvious the police were a bit fearful. I felt an increased feeling of excitement as I anticipated getting in the back seat of the auto with a raving druggie. After saying a quick prayer, I marched to the car. The police officers quit yelling as they eagerly watched to see what would happen. I opened the car door and in the softest, quietest voice I could manage, began talking to him. I sympathized with him for his injured leg. When I told him it must surely be causing him much pain, he became quiet and agreed with me. I informed him I would be happy to give him a shot to help him become more comfortable. He cooperated beautifully. He was quiet. The police were quiet. My heart was pounding. I was so thankful everyone was safe. The doctor came when the crisis was over.

Mental Illness

A small rural hospital is a poor place for the care of mentally ill people. We got them anyway. The doctors seemed to refrain from sending hometown people to a state facility or to a physician trained in the care of these patients. Surely, we could help them. Sometimes they actually improved in our little hospital. One night, a wild, raving woman was brought into the hospital. The doctor actually accompanied the family. She was screaming and waving her arms furiously. The doctor, two nurse aides, and I could not physically control this lady. The doctor gave me an order to give an injection deep in the muscle. It was a potent sedative. This lady was fully dressed. The only skin visible was her face. I quickly fixed the shot while the struggle continued with the poor woman – and poor care givers. I hurried into the room, armed with my loaded syringe and needle. I was ready and asked them to bare the bottom of our very uncooperative patient. Impossible! She was becoming more violent and the doctor didn't pretend to be a boxer or wrestler. He was getting weary and impatient – to put it mildly. He told me to give the shot through her clothes. I said I couldn't. It would not be sterile and I wasn't taught that way. The woman was winning the struggle against her three "enemies". The good doctor yelled, "Give the shot." I gave the shot. It went through three layers of clothes right into the proper place. She felt it, quit yelling, and glared at me. Believe me, that was the only time I ever gave an injection through clothing. I just knew she would have a terrible infection and I would be in deep trouble. In fifteen minutes she became quiet and never showed any sign of an unusual nursing procedure. With a little medication and follow-up treatment, she became a very docile patient.

Not all "mental" patients were violent. At times they were simply out of touch with reality. One attractive young gal would often just like to wander about in the hall. She had trouble sleeping, but remained cooperative. As I was driving to work one night, I enjoyed viewing a big, beautiful full moon in the eastern sky. Shortly after getting the night report, one of my favorite nurse aides accompanied our wandering patient down the east hall. When they got to the door, our young woman insisted on stepping outside. She just wanted to enjoy the nice night air and scenery. The aide agreed and they stepped outside. This female gazed at the full moon, raised her head, and let out this loud, long, wailing noise. It was like a wild animal baying at the moon. Eerie! My helper hurried in with her charge, taking her to her room. My shaken aide reported the incident to me and we both wondered if she was "possessed".

Melinda and I were working the night shift together. She was young and quite enjoyable to work with. We had a middle-aged man on the heart monitor following a heart attack. He appeared stable, but his electrolytes or chemical system became unbalanced. He went "bonkers" and acted like a mental patient. We made a quick call to the physician for help. Then it took both of us to try to subdue this suddenly wild man. We were so fearful he would have another attack. We definitely wanted to keep him connected to the monitoring system. We certainly learned that he was not weak! In our attempts to protect our patient, we forgot to protect ourselves. He doubled his fist and landed a powerful uppercut to Melinda's chin. I saw her head flop back, and heard her teeth crack together. I was very concerned for her welfare. She was young. She was tough. She kept insisting she was just fine. The patient responded well to the I.V. medication. The night finally ended. Our director of nurses insisted I make a full incident report in case our young nurse needed dental treatment. We were so thankful that she was not knocked out.

Sibling squabbles and fights are certainly not uncommon. It probably started with Cain and Abel. One fight occurred about midnight. A sixteen-year-old girl took on her eighteen-year-old brother. They were a couple of rough characters that the medical people were acquainted with. It started with a verbal dispute, but soon erupted into a free-for-all. Fists were flying. The female received a black eye with a small laceration. Her brother wasn't satisfied and proceeded to take a wild swing at her with his fist. She successfully evaded his right-handed thrust which caused his hand and arm to go through the glass window of the door. Even though they were both drunk, it was easy to see that the large laceration in his hand and wrist needed attention. He came blustering into the E.R. cursing and swearing – and bleeding all over the place. The doctor arrived and we began the repair work. Then things got quite interesting. His drunken sister entered the E.R., also cursing and swearing. She was barefoot, clad in a very sheer, shortie nightgown, PERIOD. It was amazing how quickly so many police officers appeared. They were obviously enjoying the scenery, unable to take their eyes off the young girl. She seemed quite happy to strut back and forth in front of them. I quickly got a hospital gown, made her put it on, and told the police they could wait elsewhere. This was not the last time I cared for this young man in our emergency room.

About one o'clock one morning a few months later, two truckers came into the E.R. drive. They had found a young man several miles west of town on Highway 50, wandering around a vehicle which had been wrecked. They looked for other people who might have been in the car, then brought the injured boy in. He was high on drugs, which did not seem to relieve the pain from a broken arm. He would not allow the truckers to assist him into the hospital and proceeded to fall flat on his face, causing a deep cut across the jaw area. Of course, the highway patrol was notified, and the Stafford police were there in force. His father was called. The emergency room was filled with men: the doc, two truck drivers, highway patrol, policemen, and the dad. I was the only female in the room. I have never heard such profanity and foul language in all my life. The doctor told the injured kid very firmly to quit talking like that – there was a lady present. It took several strong men to help hold him down while the cast was placed on the fractured arm. Then the boy became quiet and called for his father. He took his father's hand and sobbed, saying, "Oh, Dad, I have made such a mess of things." His dad was hard, uncaring, cold, and did not utter one word. For the first time I felt sympathy for this troublemaker. If only his dad had said a kind word. I have thought of this young man several times since then. You see, about five years later, he was in Texas, got into a fight, and was shot and killed. What a wasted life!

He was a well-known, loved businessman. Everyone was pleased with his work and enjoyed his pleasant personality. His daughter had been tragically injured in an auto accident and was severely brain damaged. He and his wife tenderly cared for her in their home. He began to forget important things, and the quality of his work began to deteriorate. His condition worsened rapidly. He was diagnosed with Alzheimer's disease and had to quit work.

His bizarre behavior at home was soon more than his wife could handle, since she was forced to earn a living. The local physician was aware of the entire situation in the home and was determined to keep this husband and father at home. That meant hospitalization in our facility. What an ordeal that turned out to be. He was busy every minute. He took every thing apart in the room. Blinds, drapes, soap dispensers, bathroom fixtures, closet doors, call lights, drawers – etc. were removed, taken apart, and really worked over. The maintenance man did a remarkable job successfully making electrical outlets, etc., safe. We had a terrible time trying to keep him in his room. We couldn't lock the door and certainly did not want to tie him down. I began to dread going to work. It seemed that man never slept. In fact, we had a real challenge just getting him to lie on the bed. Of course, he constantly removed all bed linens, so when we wanted to get him in bed we had to quickly remake the bed. One night, I decided to try something different. When I finally got him in bed, the only way he would be even remotely quiet was for me to hold his hand. If he would just close his eyes! Then I started to sing hymns. (I was sure he would not be aware that I am no singer.) His body became less active and agitated. I sang on and on and on, old familiar hymns. His eyes stayed open, but he was quiet. Then he sang a song with me. What harmony! Then I suggested that we pray. My earnest prayer was for him to sleep. Then he closed his eyes and began his own prayer. It was lengthy and sounded like a memorized, ritualistic prayer. All that time his eyes remained closed. He actually spent part of that night in his bed and almost seemed to sleep. Each night after that, if my time and duties permitted, we had our hymn fest and prayer. His physical condition deteriorated and he eventually died. The entire room that he had occupied had to be redone and some things replaced. Several years later, after I retired, I was helping Aunt Alice with some business. It required a meeting with this man's widow. We visited. She knew I was a nurse and had cared for her husband. I had a sudden urge to tell her of our singing and praying together. When I finished relating this information to her, she stared at me and said nothing for what seemed like ages. My heart sank. I thought I should never have told her those things. Still looking into my eyes, she very softly whispered, "I am so glad you told me." So was I.

It was a slack time in the hospital. The patient load was low, so the administrator wanted to cut down on help. Our director of nurses insisted on keeping two R.N.s on the night shift in case of a sudden emergency, so one other nurse and I were working without a nurse-aide. One of our patients was an older lady suffering from Alzheimer's disease. She was also being treated for pneumonia. Our shift was just beginning when she became extremely disturbed and agitated. It took both of us to attempt to control her. She started to fight us in a wild, vicious manner. It was difficult for one of us to leave to notify the doctor, because it placed the other one in danger. Oh, how we wished for a nurse-aide. Giving the medication that the doctor ordered was a real challenge. I received deep scratches on my arms from the wrist to the elbow. They bled a small amount. Then she grabbed my watchband and pulled. I quickly pleaded for her not to break my watch. She screamed that that is just what she intended to do – and she did. She was hitting and kicking violently. She knocked the other nurse half way across the room with a powerful kick to the chest. She became quiet before our shift ended, possibly from exhaustion. The nurses were certainly exhausted. We suggested to the administration that if they wanted to cut down on help to cut office personnel, kitchen help, laundry and cleaning people, lab, anyone except nursing staff. Did they listen? NO. The sad part of this episode for me was the fact this patient was from my hometown and was a sweet, loving person when she was well. Later the other nurse had to have a breast biopsy from the injury she received; it had not healed. We were thankful that had a happy ending.

Our hospital at Stafford had just instigated its own ambulance service. Several people in the general area had been trained and educated in first aid, C.P.R., initial assessment of patients, transporting injured and ill, giving O$_2$ therapy, etc. Most of them were strong, intelligent, dependable, and compassionate. It started quite well. The first few calls were relatively simple. Two of my favorite ambulance attendants were young men who were very tender and caring. One was married to one of our nurses; the other was special to me since I had helped deliver his first-born child. Of course, at that time, 911 was not in use. The calls for the ambulance all came through the hospital. Since there were no office personnel working at night, it was the duty of the R.N. to alert the ambulance crew.

A call came in about 2:30 a.m. from the Highway Patrol. They needed the ambulance for a burn victim from an auto accident. It was about 5 miles east of Stafford on Highway 50. My two favorite young men were on call and responded extremely fast. I quickly gave them some things I thought might be beneficial for them to give immediate care. I waited and waited for their return. I had the E.R. fixed with everything I could imagine needing to care for a dreaded burn patient. Nothing. No word. No ambulance "boys". Finally, about 5:00 they came in the back door and immediately went into the utility room and began washing things. Since they didn't even speak, I went to ask where our patient was. They both looked pale, almost green, and seemed rather ill. They simply said they had taken the victim to the mortuary. They had a strong odor of burned flesh on them. They did not talk, just cleaned linen and equipment. I have never seen anyone so stricken. At 7:00 the R.N. wife came to work. This attractive young gal came up to me, rolled her eyes, smiled weakly, and said she had really goofed when her hubby got home. She knew he had been out much of the night, working hard, so was surely hungry. She had fixed a nice breakfast with FRIED EGGS. She soon found out why it made him sick. We had gotten no information about the accident. After giving my report, I started home. Five miles east of town, I had to slow down. I saw evidence of the accident. There were several cars pulled off the roadway. Numerous men were walking up and down the ditches and into the tree row. They were obviously searching for something. It was not until I returned to work that I heard who was killed and an important detail. The man, a known drunkard, was returning to Stafford at an extremely high rate of speed when he lost control. The vehicle burned. The man was decapitated before his body was burned. All those men walking the roadside, ditches, etc. were unable to find the head of this poor man. Now I could understand why the ambulance fellows were sick. The widow was a lovely lady and handled the unpleasant situation exceptionally well. The following summer, a farmer was plowing his wheat stubble after harvest, when he made a gruesome discovery. Finally, it was found.

Violence

Violence in a larger city like Wichita could perhaps be expected, even in the late forties. In the small towns of Kansas it was very rare. Stafford was a peaceful, safe town consisting of many church-going families. Violence and crime were almost unheard of the first years of my nursing practice. As the use of illegal drugs increased, crime also became more common. Some of these crimes were frightening, sad, and hard to understand.

A young man was brought into the E.R. by some of his extremely excited buddies. It was easy to see that he was in big trouble. He was barely able to walk even with the assistance of two friends. As soon as I met them, they let go of him. I grabbed him as he started to fall. These boys were so scared I thought they were going to leave. I begged them to assist me in lifting him to the E.R. table. At first, they hesitated to answer my questions. They were panic stricken. With reluctance, they admitted he had been stabbed. The young man told me he thought he had just been kicked in the back. Quick removal of some clothing revealed a stab wound in the lower right back. There was almost no bleeding externally, but I knew he must have been losing blood internally because of rapidly decreasing blood pressure. I.V. fluids were initiated and he was transferred to a nearby hospital under the care of a surgeon. The weapon had entered the right kidney and did considerable damage. He survived and soon left Stafford to

137

live out West. To my knowledge, no one was ever arrested or punished for the act of violence.

We often heard fellow nurses say that nothing good happened after midnight. I was beginning to really believe this. Late one night in the little town of Stafford, there were two groups of kids on the streets. Surely we could not call them gangs, just two groups who were having some differences. They parted company, but were still not far from each other on the same street. One group of boys was armed with bows and arrows – the real deer hunting types. They shot some arrows at the rival group. Wow, this caused great anger! One of this angry group happened to have a gun in his possession and decided to retaliate with his weapon. He shot twice. When they saw one of the enemy fall, they ran and ran. It was almost two o'clock. June Peacock had worked the 3-11 shift and was working overtime to finish charting, etc. How thankful I was that she was there. When the young boys reached the hospital with their severely injured friend, he was already in a grave condition. It seemed the doctor was slow. June saw the serious problem and the dilemma I was in. Being a true and faithful nurse, she immediately began to help me. We worked fast. We discovered the entrance wound in the left abdomen. The M.D. made a rapid assessment and called the ambulance for a quick transport to Pratt and good surgeons. The patient was going into shock. June was very adept at starting I.V.s and proceeded to do so. I was removing his jeans and shorts so I could place a urinary catheter. It was then we discovered a second bullet wound. This one was over the lower bladder area. June and I learned that night to examine the entire body for gunshot or stab wounds. With I.V. fluid pouring into his body and a fast ambulance trip to waiting surgeons and surgical personnel, the boy survived. I often see June at church and recall our exciting night. I am still thankful for June, her expertise and her willingness

Violence

to work hours overtime with no extra pay. That is what nursing is all about.

It was almost time to feed the babies in the nursery. There were only two, but it did take time, so we usually started at 1:45 a.m. A telephone call interrupted our plans. An extremely agitated, frantic woman called informing me that they were bringing a seven-year-old boy over – fast. He had been shot. My mind was racing, as was my heart. A seven-year-old – shot at 1:45 in the middle of the night? I thought this couldn't be possible. I immediately called the physician, hoping he would be available when the family arrived. He wasn't. I kept thinking it surely would not be very serious. Perhaps the doctor thought the same thing. Remembering the hysterical woman, I met the pick-up truck in the ambulance driveway. A woman was holding the small boy on her lap. I took him from her arms to carry him into the hospital. It was summertime. He had only a pair of jeans on. As I carried him into the emergency room, I felt blood on my hand and arm that was supporting his back. His eyes were closed. His body was blue. His respirations were coming in short shallow gasps, about eighty per minute. We started oxygen to help him breathe. I saw this bullet hole in his chest. It looked like it was exactly over his heart. I looked at my nurse aide and groaned, "Oh, Verna, he's not going to make it." That's when he opened his eyes and whispered with much effort, "I want my mommy." I was so sorry that I spoke before realizing he was conscious. The doctor arrived and called for x-rays to determine where the bullet had done its damage. The couple who brought him in were his aunt and uncle. The doctor wanted to transfer him to Wichita immediately by helicopter. I needed information first – name, age, parents, etc. The aunt was so utterly distraught, she could hardly speak. She wasn't sure of his real name, he went by a nickname. She couldn't remember how old he

139

was. Her sister had just remarried and she was unable to give us her new last name. The dispatcher in Wichita said they HAD to have this information. The chopper was on the way while we continued to try to get vital facts. In the meantime, the x-ray showed that the bullet had entered over the heart in an upward direction. It tore through his left lung and shattered his left collarbone. The doctor gave attention to the poor responsible aunt. He put his arms around her shoulders to attempt to console and quiet her. He helped her place a call to her sister. What a terrible ordeal for this woman to try to explain what was going on at that hour of the night. These boys had been playing in a boyish, rowdy way. They were jumping on the bed. One boy found this rifle and was just playing with it. Because of the jumping, and the position of the "shooter", the bullet entered at an extreme angle, missing his heart. The helicopter medical people were exceptionally good with this little fellow. He had surgery that night and did recover. Someone else took care of the hungry babies in the nursery. What a night!

That same small town was again the setting of gun play. Two 18 or 19-year-old males delighted in teasing the much younger children of a nearby family. Day or night, they repeatedly teased, tormented, and frightened these kids. No one seemed to come to the assistance of these children. One night after dark, these youngsters were being chased and mistreated by the big boys. One of the pre-teen boys decided enough was enough. He found a gun, took aim, and fired. One of the tormentors was mortally wounded. He was brought into our hospital in grave condition. He had enough strength to loudly curse and swear about what happened, berating his young assailant. Despite extreme heroic efforts, this agitator died. His final breath was used taking God's name in vain. Sleep did not come easily for the nurses following their shift.

Rules and Regulations

For patient safety and efficiency a hospital must have a few rules and guidelines. When patients were to be admitted for surgery, explicit instructions were given ahead of time. Because of the use of general anesthetics, it was important for the person to have nothing to eat or drink for 12 hours. If these instructions were not followed, there was danger of vomiting with the possibility of foreign particles entering the lungs. Of course, it could cause death. Important rules.

One morning at 6:00 a.m., I admitted a man for abdominal surgery. In filling out the necessary papers for admission, I asked the important question, "Have you had anything to eat or drink since 7:00 last night?" In a rather cocky manner, he informed me that he had just finished his favorite breakfast – a big one. My next question was to determine if he had received instructions about not eating. Of course he had, but no blankity-blank nurse was going to tell him what to do. I decided it was time to turn this patient over to his physician.

Some people appreciate guidelines and rules and try to follow them, especially realizing the consequences. And there are folks who hate to take orders from anyone, like the above individual. At about that same time, I admitted a cute, sweet, little girl who was scheduled for a tonsillectomy. I noticed she appeared a bit apprehensive, so I sat down to visit for a few minutes before filling out the admission sheets. When I began writing up the admission papers, I had to once again ask that important question, "Have you had anything to eat or drink since supper last evening?" She waited a few minutes, became very serious, and her eyes grew large. She almost whispered her answer, "Oh, I swallowed my spit." I tried to be as serious as she was while I reassured her that she really had not broken a rule.

Our hospital had to have strict rules for surgery and obstetrics concerning sterile technique. We allowed no one into the birth rooms without covering clothes with a gown and shoes with "booties". One evening an obnoxious father-to-be attempted to ignore rules and charge into the birthing area. The nurse, Geri, intercepted him, again explaining the guidelines. He created quite a scene. Geri remained firm and stood her ground. Much to his wife's dismay, he argued, becoming irate. Turning the air blue with his foul language, he finally left, striding down the hall, through the lobby, and out the front door. He was gone for some time while his wife was making him a father. He finally returned to the hospital and seemed quieter – almost smug. Later, when Geri had finished her work, she prepared to drive home. It was late. Her car was parked close to the front door. She thought she smelled gasoline when she crawled into her vehicle. Dealing with people of this nature causes a deep weariness. She was eager to get home and into bed. It was a cold night and she was glad to park in the garage and get into the house. The next morning, her husband needed the car. He entered the garage and immediately detected a very strong odor of gasoline. Then he saw a large pool of gas on the floor of the garage. They were so thankful they had created no spark to cause an explosion. Upon examination they discovered the gas tank had been punctured with a sharp instrument, perhaps an ice pick. Now how could that have happened?

We had further dealings with this man, always of a similar nature. Oh, how we dreaded seeing him come into the hospital!

After extensive abdominal surgery, surgeons leave explicit orders which nurses and patients are supposed to religiously adhere to. A lady was diagnosed with cancer of the upper intestine. The surgeon successfully removed the tumor. A tube was placed through her nose, through the stomach and into the upper intestine. The doctor wanted this area to be completely empty and at rest for several days. This 78-year-old woman was patient as we gave her complete nourishment through a large vein under the collarbone. She seemed to be making a nice, but time consuming recovery. She became tired of this tube into her stomach area. It was irritating to her, so she asked the surgeon to remove it. Oh, no! It should be down three more days. The surgeon did not feel encouraged with her prognosis because of her age and the size and place of the tumor. He wanted to be very thorough and give her every opportunity to survive. The tube was kept in the proper place by a small-inflated bulb at the end of the gastric tube. She begged the doctor to remove the tube, but again he assured her it was not time for the removal. So, early in the night, she took things into her own hands. Taking a firm grasp on the "nasty, irritating, disgusting tube", she started pulling. When her task was complete, she turned on her call light. Imagine my surprise when I entered her room to find this messy tube with bulb still inflated lying across what had been nice clean bedding. Even though there was much blood coming from her nose, she triumphantly announced that the tube was out. You should have heard the attending physician! In spite of the apprehension expressed by the doctor, this lady recovered rapidly. According to lab reports, this woman was not expected to live six months. I saw her again when she was in her eighties, just as spry and feisty as ever.

A rather attractive woman in her late fifties was admitted for some serious stomach complaints. She was a widow and had no family in the area. Initial diagnostic tests showed a stomach tumor. Immediate surgery was necessary. Following surgery, the doctors came to the nurse's station and were depressed. The cancerous tumors were large and very extensive. They could not be removed. The surgeon did not expect her to recover enough to even leave the hospital. He ordered a very strict diet, definitely no coffee. He wanted her to be as comfortable as possible and did not want the stomach area irritated. She was recovering from the surgery itself, but was getting hungry. The local doctor explained the problem and the prognosis. She accepted it rather gracefully, but told him she would like to disregard the dietary restrictions. He did not think it advisable, but she did it anyway. It was springtime. She had an east room. Early in the morning, it was beginning to get light. Her call light came on. Her request was unusual. She asked if I would join her with a good cup of hot coffee, sit in her room and listen to the birds sing. I did. Never before had I really appreciated the happy sounds of the birds as dawn was breaking. She didn't have long to live, but was certainly enjoying the most simple things in life. Each morning she received her cup of coffee. I can still hear her say, "Just listen to the birds with me." She did get to leave the hospital and lived longer than the surgeon expected. I was glad I had the privilege of helping her break a "rule".

Unwinding

Working in a hospital, even a small one, can sometimes be extremely exciting, tense, tragic, perhaps exhilarating. Following such events, if at all possible, the attending physician and nurses would sit down together to talk, discuss the happenings, and maybe even weep a little. Often we would find ourselves simply encouraging one another. One night, in spite of a valiant, exhausting effort, our patient died. My co-worker nurse friend made a quick exit to the restroom to cry. The doctor was aware of her emotional turmoil. He and I sat down at the nurse's station to visit and unwind. He wanted to give an encouraging word to the nurse. She finally came out to join us. She blamed herself for not moving fast enough, perhaps not responding to a critical situation fast enough. The doctor repeatedly assured her she had acted properly. After discussing things and trying to relax, she finally told us that this patient died just like her father. She was reliving his recent death.

At times, it was the nurses that had to encourage the doctor. A middle-aged, active, vibrant, personable woman was being treated in our hospital for extremely high blood pressure and erratic heart beat. The attending physician was reasonably new to the community and was not well acquainted with this lovely lady. I had a young nurse working with me that night. The doctor was doing a remarkable job ordering the medications which should

145

reduce the blood pressure. This gal wanted to talk but the doctor thought she should be quiet and sleep. That would surely help bring the pressure down. She did go to sleep. The young nurse checked her pressure often. Fifteen minutes had elapsed, time for another check of blood pressure. My nurse friend came running out of the room in a real panic. There was no blood pressure or pulse! The doctor was there fast, but nothing could be done. What a shock! My young friend had very little experience with this type of thing. I remembered similar times when I was young. I offered to take over and make the necessary phone calls and meet the family. She appeared relieved and quickly accepted my offer. Then it was the doctor who seemed devastated. So, once again we sat down to talk things over. I even suggested to this M.D. that perhaps this was God's way of preventing this most energetic, vivacious woman from becoming a stroke invalid. With her personality, she would have had a terrible time being incapacitated.

P. was a dear nurse friend of mine. She was older and had retired. She suffered from chronic lung problems which were affecting her heart. We thoroughly enjoyed visiting with each other. About the only time we got to share a good visit was when her physical condition would cause her to be admitted to our hospital. She slept poorly, so we both anticipated our good visit as soon as I completed my initial rounds and work. Then I would head to her room for some warm conversation. I got to work one night to discover that P. had been admitted for the usual problem. When I made rounds she was asleep. The oxygen must have already helped her. She was breathing reasonably easy with her hands folded over her chest. She looked peaceful. Since she usually didn't sleep well, I returned to her room sooner than normal, anticipating our visit. She was lying in exactly the same position, but was not breathing. I immediately went for my most dependable, trusted nurse aide. I really needed someone else with me to determine if she was really gone. She was. That was one of my more difficult times. The doctor was very sympathetic. He sat down with me and helped me through a tough time. Since she had not even moved her hands, he assured me that her passing was easy and pain free. I wrote to her only daughter who lived some distance away and explained my feelings and our relationship. Several days later, I received a phone call. It was a bit of a shock at first, because it sounded just like P. talking to me. The daughter, whom I had never met, and I had a wonderful, lengthy visit.

The nurses who worked in Stafford Hospital were a very close-knit group. There were few personality conflicts. We seemed to share a common love, admiration, and respect for one another. We thoroughly enjoyed working together, playing together, and occasionally partying together. It was not unusual to share family joys and problems. Consequently, we were all aware of the health problems of a popular nurse's husband. He was a middle-aged professional man, well known in the community. At the suggestion of the local physician, this man visited a heart specialist, who came to Stafford regularly from a clinic in Wichita. After an examination, this doctor scheduled a stress test to be done in our hospital while he was present. During the test, this patient suddenly collapsed and died unexpectedly. What a shock! Of course, the wife was there. The doctors immediately escorted her into the chapel. Two of her best nurse friends were on duty and seemed unable to continue to function as nurses. In trying to deal with their own shock and grief, they were attempting to assist our dear friend with her sudden emotional turmoil. All other patients and their possible needs were quickly forgotten. All hospital activity seemed to come to a complete standstill. Soon the hospital administrator appeared, took the nurses by the arms, and reminded them they were professionals with other patients and other responsibilities. "Get back to work, NOW." With heavy hearts, they did.

Desperate Needs

People need people. Some people need help with personal care. Occasionally, we were made aware of this with brief encounters with needy humans. A mentally slow but pretty woman was brought to our facility one afternoon. Bathing? Shampoo? What are those things? This woman apparently did not have a comb or know what that was. Not only was her hair in need of shampooing, we could not get a comb through it. We tried and tried. Finally we decided to wash it, then try a comb. Still impossible. One of the nurse aides on my shift was also a beautician. We decided to cut the hair short enough to get a comb through it. That worked. She actually looked rather cute.

A similar case involved an older man. Even though he did not walk, his feet were becoming extremely sore and painful. Now this took some real old-fashioned nursing care. We had not actually seen anything like this. His toenails were thick and course. They had grown so long they grew out and curved down and back into the soles of his feet. They looked like eagle claws. The large toenails had entered the feet near the center of the arch and determinedly kept growing. He had deep, open, bleeding lesions on each foot. Soaking his feet for a lengthy time was necessary before the nail trimming could begin. After his feet healed, he was very happy. He thought he could enjoy walking again. He wasn't limber and agile enough to

149

regularly trim his nails, so someone was found who was willing and capable of doing a kind deed for this fellow.

Obesity! What a sad problem for some people. A lady in her late fifties was in desperate need of medical care. She was too large for her family to get her into a car to bring her to the hospital. Her relatives decided to place her in the back of a pick-up truck to transport her to our facility. We were warned! They drove into the emergency driveway. Now, what? The gurney certainly would not work. There was no wheel chair nearly large enough. A hospital bed was wheeled into the driveway. With family members and hospital personnel, she was finally transferred to the bed and into a room. I felt so sorry for her. Her body completely filled the bed and actually hung over both sides. So far, so good. An attempt was made to raise the head of the fine electric bed. It broke with quite a thud. Some of the old beds which had hand cranks for raising the head and knees had been kept in the storage shed. They were used for nurses to practice extinguishing fires in our regular fire drills. That became her bed. One person had difficulty raising the head of the bed by turning the handle at the foot of the bed. The doctor wanted us to get her weight, which was a reasonable and necessary order. Our scales only went to 350 pounds. Now what? We borrowed a scale from the doctor's office. Then an attempt was made to balance her on both scales at the same time. It was far from accurate. This patient was a real challenge. I can understand why she was so very quiet.

A pleasant lady was a widow, living alone. She had many friends but no one called her daily. It really did not seem necessary. One winter night, she got up to go to the bathroom. A stroke incapacitated her, causing her to fall to the floor. Her mind was clear and she could speak. She was unable to move her right arm and leg. She was a large, fleshy lady. She made a gallant struggle to try to reach the telephone. She tried in vain for three days and nights. Of course, she was soon lying in her own urine and excretion. She got cold lying on the floor. Trying to scoot or move her hips merely caused the body wastes to rub into and irritate her flesh. She was determined, and continued to struggle. Finally, a friend became concerned about her absence and discovered her terrible predicament. Her hospital stay was lengthy. The flesh on the affected hip turned black and I do mean black. It had lost the blood supply and "died". Each day more flesh would slough off. The wound became deeper and deeper. We mediated it often. After some time, we could actually see the bone. When nice pink flesh was finally visible, skin grafting was successful. After this tragic experience, many residents checked on each other daily. Yes, people need each other.

It was a cold winter night. An ice storm in the afternoon caused driving conditions to be very difficult. It would have been nice to stay at home, yet I was excited anticipating the challenge of the sixteen-mile drive to work. I left early, drove slowly, and arrived with no trouble. We all thought it would be a quiet night with such miserable weather conditions. Of course, we should never think such things. The call came well after midnight from the ambulance attendant. They were bringing a middle-aged lady in for emergency care. Be ready! They had found her on the floor in her home surrounded with copious amounts of fresh blood from a gastric hemorrhage. She had given the name of her physician in Stafford. We had no doctor by that name. I guessed at a name that sounded similar and called. It was the correct one. The patient arrived first. I saw the whitest, most colorless living person I had ever seen. I made a quick call back to the doctor to please hurry. The physician told me he had seen this woman for the first time recently and discovered a severe stomach problem. He had written a report to her, telling her to come for an appointment. No response. He was concerned, so he sent a registered letter. She still did not keep an appointment. We worked frantically. Calls were made to lab girls. She was typed and cross-matched for blood. We had two units available and started it as quickly as possible. Since she had no blood pressure, she was placed on the heart monitor for constant vitals. Surgery was necessary. The surgeon from Pratt was called and he started the icy trip to our hospital. Surgery girls were notified. When I said, "Please hurry", they knew it was a desperate situation. We were thankful they lived close because of weather conditions. We were losing the battle. We needed more blood. I called Great Bend for two units which they happened to have on hand. A Kansas Highway Patrolman successfully traveled the slick road and arrived just as the first two units were being completed. Perfect! But it was easy to see we needed more. Surgery had started. I placed a call to Hutchinson hospital for blood. Again they called on a patrolman to bring two more units. It was icing again. We wondered if he could make it. He did, again just as the others were finishing. Surgery was progressing well when the husband arrived. He reported that he had been too sleepy to come right away. Yes, he desired his rest while his wife, doctors, nurses, lab gals, and patrolmen were valiantly striving to save her life. We soon found that he was indeed a strange man. After the successful surgery to stop the stomach bleeding, the doctor questioned the husband. He asked about the registered letter, which warned them of the serious nature of his wife's ailment. He received no good answer. This was certainly a strange man. This husband received a very stern lecture from the attending physician with instructions for follow-up care. The rather pretty lady recovered and was dismissed from the hospital. The doctor never saw them again. About one year later, we read her obituary notice in the paper. Oh, well, we tried. We nurses often visited about this rather wild night when everything worked together so well – except the patient and her husband.

Abuse

Early in my nursing career I encountered neglect; but blatant abuse was very rare. Nursing responsibilities changed, became more technical and demanding. It was necessary for nurses to have continuing education. This often included legal advice. Of course it was extremely important to have liability insurance. We could be sued for millions of dollars. We had to attend classes concerning abuse, how to recognize it and the law which required us to report ANY suspicious incident that MIGHT be abuse. When I entered nursing school, I certainly wasn't expecting this to be a part of my job. It became too common.

A kindly grandfather was baby-sitting two grandchildren. A little four-year-old girl was brought into the E.R. and later admitted as a patient. She had scalding burns across the genital area of her body. They looked severe. It was explained by Grandpa. She was getting him a cup of HOT coffee. I cared for her and tried to relieve her pain. When I gave report the next morning, the R.N. immediately gasped, "Didn't you think of abuse?" I didn't. I learned a lesson. But I always hated to be suspicious. It was necessary.

A seven-month-old infant was admitted to our hospital. She was more the size of a two or three-month-old. Failure to thrive was hardly a diagnosis. Each time we changed her diaper, she screamed. We tried to be very tender and gentle and talk to her first. Her eyes appeared penetrating and fearful. A call to the physician got results. He ordered x-rays. This baby had a fractured femur. No wonder she screamed when we moved her legs for a diaper change. When the doctor visited with the parents, he became suspicious. More x-rays were ordered. She had several healed fractures, including one of the skull. Interrogation of the parents caused belligerence from the father and copious tears from the mother. Since this family had recently moved to the community, nothing was known of their past. It didn't take long to discover that twice previously, children had been removed from that home because of abuse. Proper authorities were notified and responded. The mother was quite upset and seemed to genuinely care for her infant daughter. The father emphasized his speech with profanity. NO ONE was going to take another baby away from them. The doctor would not dismiss the baby to anyone until she began to heal and start to gain weight. That is when the angry dad made his threat. He planned to come to the hospital at night, rescue his baby, and do away with any nurse who tried to stop him. As a matter of fact, since he had a gun, he just might take care of the nurse first, then get his child. Oh, the joys of nursing! I received this information at eleven o'clock one night with numerous instructions. We were to keep all doors locked at all times. All drapes and blinds were to be completely closed, especially around the babies' room. Why couldn't this have been done prior to the night shift? I was informed that the police would drive by frequently. Somehow this gave me very little comfort. After securing all the doors, I began closing blinds and drapes. We had an immediate problem. The abused baby was in a room close to the nurse's station. Across the hall from the infant was one of the cardiac care rooms. We had a heart patient on the monitor. He had been critical, but was improving. He happened to be awake when I closed the drapes. He quickly turned on his call light wanting those drapes opened. The emergency driveway was close to his window. I explained that we wanted all drapes closed at night, like it was a common request. I certainly was not going to tell him the real reason. He insisted. I pleaded. When he started to have a panic attack, I opened the drapes. I certainly did not want him to have another heart attack! All night, I tried to walk especially fast when I was in or near his room. When I entered the room of the baby, I quickly closed the door. The night ended. To my relief, the father did not appear. The infant improved and was placed in a foster home. Once again, this couple had failed as parents.

The emergency buzzer sounded shortly after the night shift began. I opened the door to greet a young teenager bringing in a four-year-old girl. Neither one appeared to be ill or injured. We sat down in the emergency room to determine the reason for this midnight visit. The young lady was obviously nervous and hesitant to talk. She was a frequent baby sitter for this little girl. The mother of the child was out with her boyfriend for the night. The sitter finally expressed her concern that the child was being sexually abused by the boyfriend of the mother. I spent considerable time getting a history. The little girl had refused to "go potty" before going to bed. She shed some tears. After spending some time talking with this child, she finally told me what had been happening. The descriptive anatomy words she used would not be found in a medical dictionary, but the meaning was apparent. I called the physician. He gently questioned and examined further. We could not feel right sending her back into this unpleasant situation. The county social worker was called and immediately responded. She had foster families available. She selected the family she thought best to deal with this problem. A call was placed, but since they lived some distance away, it took time. It was getting very late and our patient was getting drowsy. The sitter was getting weepy. What would she tell the mother? The foster parents arrived and took considerable time talking with the child, trying to get acquainted. It was difficult to imagine what it would be like to be taken in the middle of the night by perfect strangers to a strange place. She seemed willing to go. It was not easy to get follow-up information on the situation. I did find out the child stayed some time in this home and fit in well with the other children. The "boyfriend" was a known, undesirable character in the community. About two months after this interesting but sad episode in the life of a night nurse, I heard that the social worker committed suicide. How sad! What a mixed-up world we live in.

Abuse. Abuse of infants and children. There is also spousal abuse. She had beautiful, long, thick black hair. It was past midnight when she entered the emergency room. She was emotionally upset with good reason. Her head and clothing were completely blood soaked. We soon discovered that her husband had broken a large glass catsup bottle over her head. It apparently took several blows before the bottle broke. The lacerations were very large, covering much of the scalp. As I was cleaning the wounds and washing her hair, she suddenly began to tremble, actually shaking violently. I immediately thought she was going into shock. It was then I discovered her husband had followed her to Stafford and had stepped into the E.R. I wasn't sure if he was sorry and concerned about the condition of his wife or if he came to finish the job. He was escorted from the room. To properly care for the numerous and large cuts, we had to begin trimming her hair. Since my night nurse aide, the trained beautician, was there, I asked the patient if she would like a professional hair cut. She agreed. The wastebasket was soon full of pretty, black hair. After many, many sutures that took a long time, I must say she looked quite nice.

Another woman had to enter the emergency room often, always at night. We became acquainted, if you could call it that. We did see her frequently. She was extremely quiet, with a cowering attitude. She was always needing treatment for injuries inflicted by her husband. He was loud, boisterous, domineering, and demanding. He showed concern for his wife and her injuries and ordered us to fix her up. She reminded me of a dog that had received a severe beating. She would never press charges and would always return home with him. The last time I remember seeing her was one of the worst. He had grabbed her by both ears, and beat her head against the wall so hard that it made a huge hole in the wall. Of course, he immediately brought her in to be "fixed up". I never saw her again. Perhaps she finally left him.

Between Here and There

Oh, the changes that fifty years bring. Driving those sixteen miles at night was rather peaceful. I could think; I could pray; I could dream. I saw many nocturnal animals; I even got to smell an occasional skunk. Opossums acted so very dumb. Raccoons were so interesting and almost pretty. I saw them often by the grove of trees east of Sylvia. I discovered that they could give the car quite a jolt if they were hit. One night I killed one, much to my dismay. The next morning on my way home, I saw a rather touching scene. Do animals mourn? I saw another coon hovering over the dead one. On my return trip that night there were two dead coons lying at the side of the road. Now that is a picture of a devoted spouse.

I saw numerous rabbits in those first few years. Cottontails and jackrabbits were plentiful. I would see an occasional coyote. In later trips west, I never saw a rabbit. Instead, I encountered a deer. I met one head-on which caused $1,200 of damage to my car. In the early 50's, one night I counted 19 rabbits in that 16 miles. In the mid 90's, during my morning trip back to Plevna, I counted 11 deer in different spots – of course no rabbits. I think I saw a cougar, even though the game officials say it is impossible. 1 ¼ miles west of Plevna, an animal ran across the road in front of the car. It was tan colored, with a long tail. It was definitely a member of the cat family and about the size of a German shepherd dog.

Large farm critters were a bit dangerous to encounter in the roadway. Thick, heavy fog was one of the weather conditions that I took special precautions with. On those occasions, I always left early and drove very slowly. One mile west of town, I was creeping along because of extremely poor visibility. I thought I saw something unusual so I stopped the car. I found myself surrounded by black cows. I could actually reach out the window and touch a cow. The car did not even touch one of the animals. My guardian angel was certainly working that night.

Inclement weather certainly gave me some exciting experiences. After driving sixteen miles in thick fog, I would arrive at the hospital exhausted and the night had not even begun! Although I knew the highway well and could identify the residents of each house along the way, I would get lost in the fog. I tried to watch for the white line on the right side of the road. Occasionally, I would notice a yellow line on the right side. Then I knew I was on the wrong side of the road. One foggy, foggy night, it seemed I had already driven forty or fifty miles when I saw evidence of a small bridge that I never remembered seeing before. I thought I had missed Stafford completely. What a feeling! My, was I glad when I finally reached the hospital and safety.

As I drive that familiar road now, it is difficult to imagine the weather related problem I encountered one night on my way to work. It had rained on and off several days. Things were saturated. Then it rained hard and long one afternoon. It had quit when I started to drive to Stafford. I wasn't concerned and went merrily on my way. Of course, I noticed the ditches were full. When I was between Sylvia and Zenith, I was stopped by a Kansas State Trooper. He asked if it was necessary for me to travel that highway. He was very understanding when I told him I was a nurse on my way to the hospital. There was a rather lengthy stretch of highway covered with fast moving water.

He thought I could make it through okay if I would do everything just right. He assured me there was someone at both ends of the "waterway" to make sure I made it without getting washed off the road or stalling out in the middle of the puddle. I remember wondering just what they would do. He gave me explicit instructions. I should get up some speed, but do not hit that water too fast! Don't slow down! IF you get through, remember that you won't have brakes till they dry out. After listening carefully to all instructions and warnings, one thought crowded out all others: it was a man telling a woman how to do something just right. You see, if I didn't make it through okay, it would certainly be my fault for not doing it properly. I made it just fine with my guardian angel on my shoulder. I even had to splash through two more small puddles before creeping into the parking lot at the hospital. No brakes. I eased the car gently against the curb. Ah, an interesting story to tell my nurse friends.

Snow! Somehow, I really enjoyed the challenge of getting to work during a serious snowstorm. I dressed for possible trouble. I rarely called in to say I was afraid of the roads. My co-workers were certainly aware of this. In fact, one late evening, they called me wondering why I hadn't called in yet to cancel my trip over. It had snowed a little at Plevna, but it wasn't bad. At Stafford, it was bad! People could not get down the streets or into the parking lot. I stayed home. Several times, when it snowed all night, there was no way I could drive home. Now that was a tough situation. Trying to sleep in the hospital during a busy day shift was impossible. One time, I decided the labor room back in the quiet, secluded area just might work. There were no O.B. patients, so I gave it a try. I barely got settled into bed when very noisy snowplows came to clean the emergency drive and parking area. They were right outside my window. There was unwanted noise all day, no sleep for me. At least I was right there ready to go to work in the same old uniform. And that is what I did.

I have been given excellent instructions on how to drive a car safely on ice-covered road – several times. I needed it. Now, remember, drive slowly. If you begin to slip, slide, skid, or spin out of control, do NOT put on the brakes! All you have to do is turn the wheel in the direction you are skidding. They make it sound simple, even though I cannot imagine turning the wheels the direction you are going when you don't want to go that way. I left for work thirty minutes early that night because of extremely icy highways. I was content to slowly creep along, gently easing my way around the curve east of Sylvia. So far, so good. Really, this wasn't too difficult. At the west edge of Sylvia, I noticed a vehicle on the blacktop road which goes south toward Turon. Just as I approached the intersection, this light brown station wagon pulled out right in front of my car. Of course, I slammed on the brakes. Then I had the ride of my life. There were five cars parked along the edge of the road. I went around that curve in a most unique fashion. When I started, I was headed west. As I followed the curve, skimming, oh so close to those parked cars, my car pointed south, then east very briefly, then north. Although I was some distance down the south road when I finally came to a stop, I was heading north, just the direction I need to go to get back on the road to Stafford. I noticed the station wagon parked at the intersection. Apparently, someone had enjoyed watching me slide by all those cars, going every direction, and not hitting one of them. Some unseen force must have kept me from smashing into a line of cars. I sat a few minutes to allow my heart rate to slow a bit before proceeding on the drive to the hospital. I also wanted that station wagon to move on out of sight. My pulse was ALMOST back to normal when I entered the safety of the hospital.

My husband was always concerned about my safe arrival on stormy nights. He gave me instructions to call him when I arrived at the hospital. You see, this was prehistoric times – no cell phones. When roads were snow packed or icy, he preferred I take Highway 50 instead of Trail West Road because it had much more traffic. It was that type of weather when I started home one winter morning. Although I preferred Trail West (I didn't like to go over the ice covered overpass on Highway 50), I took the better-traveled road. Everything went well until I turned on the dirt road to go the last mile into Plevna. All of a sudden, I started skidding out of control. I must have done everything wrong, because when I got stopped, I was in the ditch. At least I was within walking distance of home. I was carefully easing my way down the road, when I noticed a car coming behind me. I certainly didn't want anyone to stop. I was afraid if they braked, the car would slide right into me. It was Bobby Zongker. He stopped without a problem, picked me up, and took me home. Later, my husband brought the car home. It was then that we discovered some neighbor had a strange sense of humor. Wouldn't it be funny for someone to find some full and empty beer cans in the car of a Sunday school teacher, especially when the car was stalled in a snowy ditch?

It was a busy night at the hospital. A woman had undergone a serious surgical procedure, so her husband had spent the night with her. An older lady was nearing the end of her struggle with cancer. Because of this her son spent the night in her room. All during the night, the snow was coming down. The wind was blowing. Just before daybreak, the snow quit and the snowplows began their important job of opening the highways. When my work was completed, I was informed the highway was open, so I started home. I had gone only about three miles when I hit an icy spot and slid into the big snow bank at the edge of the road. The car was stuck really tight. In a matter of one or two minutes, two different men in big pick-up trucks stopped to offer help. It was the same two men who had shared my pot of coffee at the hospital during the night. They had my car out of the snow bank in no time. I'm still thankful for good friends.

Day after day, week after week, I would start that morning trip from Stafford to Plevna. I began to notice that I often met a man driving a black pick-up. I do not know who started it, but soon we were giving a friendly wave as we met on the highway. This went on for a long time. I missed the morning greeting when the black pick-up quit coming by. Months later, I was approached by a stranger who began a friendly visit. I felt that I was supposed to know him. With a brief apology, I informed him I didn't think I knew him. He smiled and said we had waved at each other for two or more years. He was a teacher on his way to work. I was a nurse on my way home from work. Nice.

In my last year of working, a truck driver friend of mine gave me a bit of information which made me consider my actions. He said he waves at all the vehicles he meets on the highway. Then he explained who waves and who doesn't wave. "Old, gray-haired women NEVER wave back." Ouch! That sounded like he was describing me. So I decided to conduct a survey of my own. When I drove those sixteen miles during daylight, I waved energetically at every vehicle I met. It was fun. I averaged the numbers after three days. Fifty percent of all car drivers waved. One hundred percent of all pick-up drivers waved back at me. Not one semi truck driver waved. Maybe they were old, gray-haired women.

Fear while driving alone at night was extremely rare. It happened once shortly after I left Plevna. A car passed me, then slowed down to about 25 miles an hour and proceeded to drive in the center of the road. I felt it was necessary to get around him or I would be late for work. I succeeded in passing him with the help of a shallow ditch. I was surprised when he soon caught and passed me. Again, he slowed down and drove in the center of the road. Then I began to feel uneasy. I decided if I could get around him again, I would certainly break the speed limit to stay ahead. That is what I did!

One summer night, I was cruising down the road, enjoying the drive. I slowed down as I was approaching the intersection west of Zenith because it looked like a fire at the edge of the road. As I slowly proceeded, I saw people moving about. I thought someone was in trouble. I almost stopped. What I saw made me to decide to drive on. I saw an almost perfect, circular fire like a big ring. There was no flame in the center. There were about 7 or 8 young men, all without shirts and shoes, dancing around the circular fire. It looked very strange. I did wonder if drugs were involved.

"Extracurricular"

Since I am a nurse, I have had the privilege of helping people in different ways. Giving weekly injections to friends and neighbors saved them driving to the city and paying a professional a tidy sum. Most of these were allergy shots, so I had to keep the extra proper medication on hand in case of a reaction. Several school teachers dropped by for their weekly injection. I enjoyed seeing little fellows once a week, even though I had to bribe one of them with a banana in order to gain cooperation. I gave occasional shots to an older lady. She had to lie down on the bed and insisted that I place a clean sheet on the bed. At one time I drove several miles to medicate a sweet lady who was dying from cancer. She was so appreciative.

For several years, I visited three different people here in town every week. I checked their blood pressures and set up all their weekly medications in an orderly fashion. Of course, they wanted me to linger a while for a nice visit. One of these friends had an artificial eye. Each week, I was to remove and clean it. One week, when I replaced it and looked at my patient, I was a bit shocked. I had put it back incorrectly. His useful eye was looking right at me. The artificial one was pointed up and out. It looked so funny, I just started laughing. When I explained it to him, he joined me in laughter. We always had a good time.

Getting enough sleep was a constant problem for me. Many of my friends and neighbors seemed to have the idea that night workers needed only a brief nap to carry on all activities. One of the most intelligent women in this community was on a school committee with me. She was in charge. I got home from working all night about 8 a.m. I went to bed as soon as possible. It seemed I could get my best sleep as soon as I got home from the hospital. At 10 a.m. the phone rang. I must have sounded sleepy, because she immediately asked if I was napping. I told her NO, I was asleep. She wanted to discuss the school project. I asked if she could call another time. I really wanted to sleep. O.K. At 12 o'clock noon, the phone rang. I sleepily answered to hear this lady ask in a shocked voice, "Are you STILL asleep?" While I was working that night, I had this terrific urge. I wanted to call this hard working woman at midnight, then again at 2 a.m. and be very surprised that she was STILL in bed. Of course, I refrained.

I had the night off and had just prepared for bed when the phone rang. A schoolteacher and his wife lived across the street and had just come home from the hospital with a newborn babe. The new mother was a bit hysterical and I could not understand her – I did not even know who it was. The father quickly grabbed the phone and said the baby had stopped breathing. I ran across the street in my night garb. When I hurried into the room, the baby was a little blue, but was beginning to breathe. I stayed a while until things appeared to be back to normal. They were relieved and happy. I had a feeling they did not go to bed very soon.

The night had been difficult and strenuous. I was so glad to be home. The boys went to school and I was eager to get to bed. Yes, the phone rang. An older lady who lived a few miles out in the country asked if I would swab her husband's throat if she brought him to my home. That request seemed a bit too much for this tired nurse. I suggested she do it. OH, she couldn't do that! Then I told her I was getting ready to go to bed – couldn't they come in the afternoon. She insisted they needed it done soon. I tried every angle to put her off. Then she got real sweet and informed me she did not want me to come to their house. She would bring him to town. I stayed up and did what I thought anyone could do. At least they did not stay and visit.

We had a pleasant, quiet neighbor lady who lived several miles out of town. She had just undergone surgery for a malignant growth in her intestine. She had to have a colostomy. She needed help and practice learning how to care for her physical problem. I received a call from her asking for help. She knew I worked nights and did not want to interfere with my rest. But she needed someone to help her every day for a period of time. We worked out a schedule that was best for both of us. She accepted her condition very well and learned quickly. Soon she was able to handle everything by herself. She and her husband certainly appreciated my help. It saved them many trips into Hutchinson.

When our three older boys were in grade school, we had a good school with a very active P.T.A. Because I happened to be the only nurse in the community at that time, the organization called on me for extra little requests of service. The first thing I was asked to do was to give hearing tests to the entire grade school. I was able to choose the time, so I missed no sleep. I was given a small secluded room which was very quiet. I found the whole project not only interesting but also fun and enjoyable.

The other request was different. For some reason which I do not remember, the entire school district, both grade and high school, needed to have skin tests for tuberculosis. The Sylvia schools also needed the tests. Of course, it was necessary for a physician to be in on the project. Our local P.T.A. sponsored and paid for the necessary medical supplies and the service of the doctor. This Hutchinson physician could not function without the help of a registered nurse. The principal asked the only available local nurse to please fill the need. The big problem for me was that it was scheduled on a day right after I had worked all night. I was assured that I could surely sleep later in the day. No one knew how difficult that was for me. I don't suppose anyone really cared. I felt obligated to say yes. My job was to set up all the medication, needles, etc., before the busy doctor arrived. Since all school employees needed the test and a few could not wait for the arrival of the physician, I gave all the early tests. When the doctor appeared, the principal greeted him like he was a king or god, practically bowing down to him. All the kids were herded through lines with the doctor and I each injecting a drop of serum just under the skin of the forearm. It went well, but the doctor had to leave before all the employees could get there. So, once again, I stayed for the latecomers, then I cleaned everything up. I got very little sleep that day but I helped the community. Three days later all the skin tests had to be read. The same doctor had to come. A nurse could help, if a physician was present. This doctor would not drive the extra six miles to Sylvia, so they had to bus all the kids to Plevna. At least I did not miss so much sleep that day. At our next P.T.A. meeting, a report was given about this successful project. The organization paid the doctor for a couple of hours and his drive out to the country. The pay for the physician was about equal to a week's pay for me. The school organization presented me with a pretty decorated bar of soap for my help in this undertaking.

Ah, one morning, I got home from work in good time and relished the thought of a good long sleep which I always seemed to need. The telephone awakened me after about thirty minutes of rest. This occurred before the "invention" of 911. When I answered the phone, a pleasant female voice spoke, informing me she was the operator. She surprised me by asking if I was a nurse. Hearing my affirmative answer, she very quickly told me I was needed immediately at a neighbor's home. I was now wide awake and leapt out of bed, dressed in double time, and hurried to the destination, not knowing what to expect. Upon arrival, I discovered a semi-conscious lad about 4 years of age. Given a quick history by the very excited mother, I felt this young boy had had an unexpected seizure. An ambulance was on the way. I remained with the family until help arrived. He was conscious and responding by then. He was diagnosed with epilepsy. Another day without enough sleep for this night nurse!

Trivia

Several years ago, there were no convenience stores in the area. Of course, in Stafford, all businesses closed fairly early. City policemen and State patrol officers knew the only place open at night was the hospital. They frequently stopped in for a welcome cup of coffee and a friendly chat. If I was not busy, I enjoyed getting acquainted with some fine law enforcement people. One year my husband and I went to the Kansas State Fair. As usual, there were many troopers there. He was quite shocked when I was warmly greeted by some of them.

One night we happened to notice that a skunk was parked right outside the emergency room door in the driveway. So often, we had people come into the drive, usually needing medical help. If anyone came at night, they considered it an emergency! I felt that we must try to get that skunk to move, but how? We watched a while. He just stayed exactly where he wanted to be - right in front of the door, so I decided to call on one of my friendly, coffee drinking police pals. The one working that night was a short, older man who always acted like he knew everything there was to know about everything. I told him our problem. He said he would be right down and take care of the situation. I was curious and watched out the window. He drove up, got out of the car with a powerful flashlight and shined it directly into the eyes of the friendly skunk. He then reached down and picked up the skunk by the tail. He held the animal out of the window and drove out of town. He soon returned and came in to report to me. He explained that a skunk is helpless if you pick it up by the tail. He didn't want to kill it, so he just took it out into the country. I thanked him as we drank coffee together.

One of the doctors that served Stafford for many years was a music teacher before he became a physician. This doctor loved music. He played the cello and often gave the special music at the church he attended. He also directed the choir. When we had our annual hospital Christmas party, he enthusiastically led the group in singing Christmas carols. One night about 3:00 a.m. the telephone rang. It was this doctor, wide-awake. He had been awakened and could not resume his sleep, so he put some classical music on his record player. He felt it was too enjoyable to not share with someone else. Making sure I was not too busy, he asked me to listen to his music with him. I thought it a strange request. Before 15 minutes passed, I was ready to quit listening, but I waited until his long-haired music was finished. Then he wanted to discuss the beautiful music we had enjoyed together. Ah, the life of a night nurse.

We were experiencing a quiet night, which was certainly welcome, since we had been rather busy. Shortly after two o'clock someone came into the emergency room. It was a young, recently married couple. I was startled to see the young girl because her mouth was wide open and she did not talk. Her husband quickly explained that she had awakened, yawned an enormous yawn, and her jaw popped out of place. She appeared utterly miserable. I must admit that it did look a bit funny to see her mouth stay open so wide. Even though I had been taught how to put a jaw back in place, I decided to call on a physician to do the job. He quickly took care of the situation without getting his thumbs bit.

Yawns. Hiccups. Both are rather common occurrences. We had one man who had hiccups for nine days. They were hard, body-jerking hiccups. I thought he might die from exhaustion. Medication did not seem to help. We could put a small rubber tube down his throat and touch a certain area and the hiccups would cease, but only for a short time. We did that procedure often at night to try to help him get some much needed rest. After nine days, relief came.

Party Time

Dr. Longwood served the Stafford area for many years. His wife, Muriel, suffered a stroke, which left her in a weakened condition. He decided to retire and moved to Arizona. Later, a group of former patients and employees planned an appreciation reception for him. All of his former employees were asked to attend. There was quite a group of nurses and other workers who enjoyed the day with him and his wife. There was an outpouring of love. I certainly enjoyed seeing many of our former patients.

I was at the hospital for a meeting one afternoon. One of the first women I had cared for years earlier met me in the hall. Her initial greeting was a shocked "Are you STILL working here?" Wow! Perhaps I should consider retirement. Some aspects of retirement certainly sounded good. Sleeping every night. Taking orders (suggestions) from my husband and son instead of a physician. Time with precious grandchildren. More social life. The list goes on. It made the decision easier since many of my good nurse friends were also considering retirement. I enjoyed my work. I loved my co-workers, but I knew it was time to make the change. The nursing personnel had a dinner party for me. I was presented with a gift and a beautiful retirement book, which is filled with wonderful memories from my dear friends.

This group of retired nurses and some that are not retired meet in Stafford every three months for dinner, visiting, laughing, and reminiscing. Our time together is filled with warmth and love.

Yes, it is party time. My Wesley nurse friends also remain faithful and close. We get together once a year in June. Our meeting in the year 2000 was especially meaningful. We celebrated the fiftieth year since our graduation from dear old Wesley. What a grand and special time we had. Some of our group had not been back since we graduated in 1950, but we recognized each other. Now we were a group of old ladies, but the energy, the laughter, the spark was still there. We spent three days celebrating. These friends will always be precious to me. I value their friendship.

Afterglow

After my retirement, I motored to Stafford once a week to spend time with my Aunt. We were in a restaurant one day and saw an elderly lady that I had cared for years ago. I wanted to speak to her. I was pleased when she recognized me. She took my hand and with much warmth, told me that all she now remembered about the death of her husband was that I was with her.

About the same time I met the sister of a patient who had received weekly injections from me. She immediately approached me to tell me what her sister thought of me. (It was good.) The sister had probably been dead for 35 years.

I went into the hospital one morning for a meeting. A woman I did not know approached me, making sure of my identity. She quickly explained her mission. I had spent many nights visiting and caring for her mother who was dying of cancer. Her mother wanted to talk about heaven. One of my co-workers felt very uncomfortable doing that. The patient and I spoke often and sometimes long discussing the subject, which was dear to her heart. I remember one thing that seemed to fascinate her was the size of the pearls spoken about in Revelation 21:21, one pearl at each gate. Her daughter handed me a book that is titled, "Heaven, a Place, a City, a Home". She told me that this was the book her mother wanted me to have. I am so glad she wrote that inside the book along with the date.

When my Mother died, I received a card and letter from a woman in Stafford. I did not recognize the name. In her letter, she explained that I had cared for her mother the night she died. She appreciated the kindness and tenderness expressed. I did not remember the patient or her daughter.

It is these expressions of thanks and appreciation which make me feel that all those years of nursing was worthwhile, after all. It helps me forget the unpleasant experiences.

Years ago, I had a dream. I wanted to become a nurse. After I read a poem, my dream seemed even more important. The poem is entitled "The Nurse", and the author unknown:

> *To be a nurse is to walk with God,*
> *Along the path that our master trod;*
> *To soothe the achings of human pain;*
> *To faithfully serve for little gain;*
> *To lovingly do the kindly deed,*
> *A cup of water to one in need;*
> *A tender hand on a fevered brow,*
> *A word of cheer to those living now;*
> *To reach the soul through its body's woe,*
> *Ah, this is the way that Jesus would go.*
> *Oh, white-capped nurses in dresses of blue,*
> *Our great Physician is working through you.*

My dream became a reality. As I look back, I realize that the salary for a professional nurse was poor. Then I remember that was not my reason for becoming a nurse. I have no regrets.

Nurse, Please!!

I have been blamed.	I have been blessed.
I have been cussed.	I have been kissed.
I have been threatened.	I have been thanked.
I have been accused.	I have been appreciated.
I have been called a demon.	I have been called an angel.

I have been a nurse.

Index

To purchase more copies of this book, please fill out the information below, and send this page with your check or money order made out to:

Plevna Publishing, L.L.C.
Book Fulfillment Department
8118 S. Avery Rd.
Plevna, Kansas 67568

Nurse, Please!! ...._____ copies @ $14.95 each = _____

Shipping and Handling ... _____ copies @ $2.00 each = _____

Kansas deliveries include 6.3% Sales Tax .... = _____

Total: _____